Once for All Delivered
to the Saints

Monographs in Baptist History

VOLUME 10

SERIES EDITOR
Michael A. G. Haykin, The Southern Baptist Theological Seminary

EDITORIAL BOARD
Matthew Barrett, Midwestern Baptist Theological Seminary
Peter Beck, Charleston Southern University
Anthony L. Chute, California Baptist University
Jason G. Duesing, Midwest Baptist Theological Seminary
Nathan A. Finn, Union University
Crawford Gribben, Queen's University, Belfast
Gordon L. Heath, McMaster Divinity College
Barry Howson, Heritage Theological Seminary
Jason K. Lee, Cedarville University
Thomas J. Nettles, The Southern Baptist Theological Seminary, retired
James A. Patterson, Union University
James M. Renihan, Institute of Reformed Baptist Studies
Jeffrey P. Straub, Central Seminary
Brian R. Talbot, Broughty Ferry Baptist Church, Scotland
Malcolm B. Yarnell III, Southwestern Baptist Theological Seminary

Ours is a day in which not only the gaze of western culture but also increasingly that of Evangelicals is riveted to the present. The past seems to be nowhere in view and hence it is disparagingly dismissed as being of little value for our rapidly changing world. Such historical amnesia is fatal for any culture, but particularly so for Christian communities whose identity is profoundly bound up with their history. The goal of this new series of monographs, *Monographs in Baptist History*, seeks to provide one of these Christian communities, that of evangelical Baptists, with reasons and resources for remembering the past. The editors are deeply convinced that Baptist history contains rich resources of theological reflection, praxis and spirituality that can help Baptists, as well as other Christians, live more Christianly in the present. The monographs in this series will therefore aim at illuminating various aspects of the Baptist tradition and in the process provide Baptists with a usable past.

Once for All Delivered to the Saints

Essays on the History of the Christian Faith
in Honor of Gerald L. Priest

EDITED BY
Michael A. G. Haykin
AND *Allen R. Mickle*
WITH *Ian Hugh Clary*
AND *Roy M. Paul*

FOREWORD BY
David M. Doran

☙PICKWICK *Publications* • Eugene, Oregon

ONCE FOR ALL DELIVERED TO THE SAINTS
Essays on the History of the Christian Faith in Honor of Gerald L. Priest

Monographs in Baptist History 10

Copyright © 2019 Wipf and Stock Publishers. All rights reserved. Except for brief quotations in critical publications or reviews, no part of this book may be reproduced in any manner without prior written permission from the publisher. Write: Permissions, Wipf and Stock Publishers, 199 W. 8th Ave., Suite 3, Eugene, OR 97401.

Pickwick Publications
An Imprint of Wipf and Stock Publishers
199 W. 8th Ave., Suite 3
Eugene, OR 97401

www.wipfandstock.com

PAPERBACK ISBN: 978-1-5326-5224-0
HARDCOVER ISBN: 978-1-5326-5225-7
EBOOK ISBN: 978-1-5326-5226-4

Cataloguing-in-Publication data:

Names: Haykin, Michael A. G., editor. | Mickle, Allen R., editor. | Doran, David M., foreword.

Title: Once for all delivered to the saints : essays on the history of the Christian faith in honor of Gerald L. Priest / edited by Michael A. G. Haykin and Allen R. Mickle, with Ian Hugh Clary and Roy M. Paul; foreword by David M. Doran.

Description: Eugene, OR: Pickwick Publications, 2019 | Series: Monographs in Baptist History 10 | Includes bibliographical references.

Identifiers: ISBN 978-1-5326-5224-0 (paperback) | ISBN 978-1-5326-5225-7 (hardcover) | ISBN 978-1-5326-5226-4 (ebook)

Subjects: LCSH: Theology, Doctrinal—History.| Baptists—Doctrines—History | Priest, Gerald L.

Classification: BX6331.3 06 2019 (print) | BX6331.3 (ebook)

Manufactured in the U.S.A. 01/31/19

Contents

List of Contributors | vii
Foreword BY DAVID M. DORAN | ix
Preface BY ALLEN R. MICKLE, JR. | xi

1. A Biography of Gerald L. Priest BY KEVIN L. PRIEST | 1
2. Publications of Gerald L. Priest | 6
3. "He Can Do It if He Will": Jonathan Edwards, Inability, and the Theologians BY JOHN ALOISI | 8
4. "He Went About Doing Good": Eighteenth-Century Particular Baptists on the Necessity of Good Works BY MICHAEL A. G. HAYKIN | 29
5. "To Declare the Whole Counsel of God": Andrew Fuller (1754–1815) on Preaching BY ALLEN R. MICKLE, JR. | 44
6. "A Young Man's Difficulty with His Bible": Not My Father's Faith BY JEFF STRAUB | 55
7. George Burman Foster: First Radical of the Chicago School BY VAN E. CARPENTER | 80
8. The Fundamentalist as Historian: The Civil War Histories of Clarence Macartney BY MARK SIDWELL | 110

Contributors

John Aloisi (PhD) is Assistant Professor of Historical Theology, at Detroit Baptist Theological Seminary, Allen Park, MI.

Van Carpenter is (MDiv, STM, MS) is a Consultant with LibraryTek and a PhD candidate in Church History at Central Baptist Theological Seminary, Plymouth, MN.

Ian Hugh Clary (PhD) is Assistant Professor of Historical Theology at Colorado Christian University, Lakewood, CO.

David M. Doran (PhD) is the senior pastor of Inter-City Baptist Church and President of Detroit Baptist Theological Seminary. He serves as the Chairman of the Practical Theology Department and teaches the core pastoral theology courses in the MDiv program.

Michael A. G. Haykin (ThD) is Professor of Church History and Biblical Spirituality at The Southern Baptist Theological Seminary, Louisville, KY and Director of The Andrew Fuller Center for Baptist Studies at Southern Seminary.

Allen R. Mickle (MDiv, ThM) is Adjunct Instructor of Bible and Theology at Clarks Summit University, Clarks Summit, PA.

Roy M. Paul (BA, BSc, MTS) is Executive Research Assistant at the Canadian office of the Andrew Fuller Center for Baptist Studies.

Contributors

Kevin L. Priest (EdD) is the School Administrator for Hampton Park Christian School in Greenville, SC.

Mark Sidwell (PhD) is Professor, Division of Social Science at Bob Jones University, Greenville, SC.

Jeff Straub (PhD) is Professor of Church History at Central Baptist Theological Seminary, Plymouth, MN.

Foreword

Dr. Gerald Priest served on the faculty of Detroit Baptist Theological Seminary from 1988 to 2010. I had the privilege of serving along side of him and of being his pastor for all but a few months of that time. Dr. Priest was a gift from God to our seminary and congregation and we are thrilled to see him honored in this way.

Gerald Priest wore many hats and wore them all well. As a professor of church history, he skillfully combined scholarship with a love for his subject matter. He helped ingrain into the culture of DBTS an awareness that we stand on the shoulders who those who preceded us and we must learn from their challenges, successes, and failures. Whether speaking in classroom, chapel pulpit, conference lectern or writing in our seminary journal, he helped craft an historical awareness that greatly helped our seminary family.

His love for history was not merely an academic pursuit, though. His zeal for genuine revival drove him to understand and retell the story of God's work in the revivals of our nation's past, and to distinguish them carefully from the shallow works of revivalists. His burden for proper, biblically-defined ecclesiastical separation led to serious, thoughtful work on the early history of fundamentalism. His love for the gospel and its spread within the home led to the production of a Baptist catechism.

Dr. and Mrs. Priest were exemplary church members who faithfully participated in the life our assembly. They lived the life that Dr. Priest was seeking to encourage in his students at the seminary. They were a blessing to this pastor!

Foreword

Beyond our congregation, Dr. Priest served our nation as a chaplain in the Army National Guard and many other congregations through faithful pulpit supply. He wore the preacher hat well and many were blessed through his faithful exposition of the Word.

Perhaps no clearer legacy of a man's ministry can be found than a desire by his former students and friends to honor him as this book aims to do. Gerald Priest reproduced his love for God, the Scriptures, Baptist history, and his fundamentalist heritage in the lives of his students. He skillfully took his place in the scholarly world with articles and lectures that benefitted the larger historical discussion. In short, he made an impact and left a rich legacy. May God be honored through this attempt to extend that legacy as a means of honoring his faithful service!

Dr. David M. Doran, Senior Pastor, Inter-City Baptist Church, Allen Park, MI & President and Professor of Pastoral Theology, Detroit Baptist Theological Seminary, Allen Park, MI

Preface

"I don't see why this is important for my ministry." And so the comment was overheard regarding the importance of studying the history of the church for the ministry of the church today. As a young seminary student at Detroit Baptist Theological Seminary I heard the comment in passing by a fellow student, with whom I could sympathize. While I grew up in a home that emphasized the importance of history, I often wondered how studying the church hundreds of years in the past would help in my ministry today as pastor. How could debates and issues that seemingly had little bearing on what was happening now help me serve my flock? We seminarians could all understand taking the biblical languages, systematic theology, and homiletics, but church history?

Enter Jerry Priest, whom I will forever call Dr. Priest. He was both my professor of church history and my professor of homiletics at Detroit Baptist Theological Seminary in Allen Park, MI. It was here, in his thorough research and careful attention to detail yet in his simultaneously winsome way, that he showed me how important it was to not just study homiletics but to study the history of the church. Through his love of both the church militant and the church triumphant, he showed us how knowing the struggles and the triumphs of the past really do have meaning for us in the here and now. I will forever be changed by his influence.

Two events, following my formal studies, stand out about Dr. Priest's interest and the impact that he has had on my life. When I told him of my desire to pursue doctoral studies in New Testament (which had been the subject of my ThM studies), he said, "New Testament PhD's are a dime

Preface

a dozen. Study church history." That became a turning point for me in seeing church history as a career I should consider. And though I began to follow his advice, I have put that pursuit on the back burner (but who knows what the future might bring), it has only caused my love for the history of the church to increase. The second event was his willingness to fly to be part of my ordination council and service. He preached wholeheartedly and challenged me to be a faithful pastor of the flock that God has entrusted to me. Through my ups and downs of ministry, Dr. Priest has been there as a faithful and caring advisor. Not only did he shape my formative thinking about church history, but he has continued to serve as a father to me in my ministry.

For these, and other countless reasons, I felt Dr. Priest needed to be honored. Sometimes the historians are forgotten rather than bestowed the honor they deserve for keeping the history of the church in front of us as we move forward. Thankfully, another historical mentor and friend, Dr. Michael Haykin, agreed to help see this honor come to fruition. Other former students and colleagues of Dr. Priest, knowing too his enormous impact on the church and its servants, agreed to help honor him as well. After a number of years, this book has finally has appeared as a meager attempt to honor our friend, colleague, and mentor. Because of Dr. Priest's enormous love for the church, and his desire to safeguard and protect its doctrine, we have determined to focus our attention upon areas that were of great interest to him, particularly areas of Baptist and Evangelical history, and the fundamentals of the faith. This means that Dr. Priest, who fulfills the very best of what it means to be a Fundamental Baptist, will hopefully find the essays in this volume a testimony to his enduring legacy.

Following a survey of Dr. Priest's life and bibliography by his son Kevin, John Aloisi, Dr. Priest's heir at Detroit Baptist Theological Seminary, picks up an area of great interest to Dr. Priest, namely the issue of moral and natural inability in the thought of Jonathan Edwards. Dr. Priest had addressed the issue previously in print, regarding Andrew Fuller's appropriation of Edward's thinking, and it is fitting that Aloisi continue to evaluate Edwards' lasting impact.

Michael Haykin then brings to bear his love of eighteenth-century Baptists to Dr. Priest's long-standing love of Baptist history. Dr. Priest would wholeheartedly embrace the notion that we should pursue a life of good works as an outflow of our salvation, just as our Baptist forebears did. In my essay, I also consider eighteenth-century Baptist life by looking at Andrew Fuller's theology of preaching. Fuller has left an indelible stamp upon the evangelical world, particularly in bringing Edwards' theology to the Baptists. What is often neglected, as scholars have focused on his theology, is his work as a churchman. Here I consider what Fuller can teach the church about preaching the Word of God. Since Dr. Priest taught me both Baptist history and homiletics, it seems only fitting to honor him in this way.

Jeff Straub's essay on the liberal Baptist William Newton Clarke reminds us that one must be aware of those with whom we may disagree theologically if we are to disseminate our own understanding to further generations. Clarke's departure from the more evangelical theology of his father and forebears, serves to show us how quickly the theological foundations can fall and the need for the church to remain vigilant in defending the gospel. Van Carpenter's work on George Burman Foster does the same as Straub's essay. The influence of liberalism began to permeate the Northern Baptist Convention, especially as disseminated through the liberal University of Chicago Divinity School. Seeing the continued departure from the faith that was once entrusted to the saints, is something we must watch for in our own institutions and churches.

Finally Mark Sidwell's interesting look into the Civil War histories of Clarence Macartney gives us a look at how a fundamentalist has done history in the past. Historiography is vitally important. As Dr. Priest is a self-confessed fundamentalist historian, consideration of how others have practiced the craft before continues to inform us on how we should do history today.

Together, while focusing on differing topics, these essays come together to honor Dr. Priest with areas of vital interest to him in the history of Christ's church. If anyone that I know has tried to communicate the importance of maintaining the theological foundations of the faith it is Dr. Priest. We hope and pray that this book would both edify the saints, but also honor the legacy of a wonderful man of God.

Allen R. Mickle, Jr.
Stanfordville, New York
February 17, 2015

1

A Biography of Gerald L. Priest

Kevin L. Priest

GERALD (JERRY) LEE PRIEST was born November 1, 1944, in Indianapolis, Indiana, to Armond Alvin Priest and Maxine (Roberts) Priest, the second of three sons. His father Armond was adopted by a Chicago businessman, who dabbled in politics. Armond did not come to know the Lord until later in life through the continued prayer and witness of Jerry during his college years, and he was not particularly involved in his sons' upbringing. Jerry remembers that his father was a hard worker, however he sometimes carried two or three jobs to provide for his family. Maxine was a graduate of Butler University and Jordan Conservatory of Music. She was an accomplished church pianist and organist and instilled a love for the arts in Jerry. In contrast to Armond, she was a cheerful spirit, nurturing, and was remembered as a constant encourager to her children. Maxine claimed to have professed Christ as a young child, and she and Armond attended a local Christian Church in Indianapolis, where they loved to sing in the choir and, she, to play the piano and organ.

Jerry came to know the Lord at the age of nine at a church-sponsored Christian camp in Indiana. He later attended Ben Davis High School and was a good student. He particularly enjoyed choir, art, and dramatic productions and was also heavily involved in the Ben Davis chapter of Youth for Christ. The regional Youth for Christ coordinator encouraged him toward what would become two profound influences during his early years.

The first was to attend the Lifegate Baptist Church of Indianapolis, pastored by Ford Porter, best known for the *God's Simple of Plan of Salvation* gospel tract. Jerry remembers Porter as a man of prayer with great compassion for the lost and who could never preach without weeping. The second was to attend Bob Jones University (BJU) in Greenville, South Carolina. When Jerry learned that the current university president was also a renowned Shakespearean actor, his interest was piqued. A personal letter from Dr. Jones, Jr. himself, describing a scholarship program and encouraging Jerry to apply, sealed the deal.

Jerry arrived on the Bob Jones University campus in the fall of 1962 to study dramatic productions; however, during the spring 1963 university Bible Conference, he surrendered to the ministry. The speakers that year included Bob Jones Sr., another major inspiration to Jerry, as well as John R. Rice, Ernest Pickering, and Robert Ketcham. Jerry attributes Ketcham with providing the greatest influence on his call to the ministry. While waiting for Ketcham to sign his Bible after one service, he fondly remembers overhearing Ketcham's wife describe her husband to another student as "the greatest man of God I've ever known." Shortly after the Bible Conference, Jerry changed his major to Bible; but after discussing the switch with his speech teacher, he was advised to continue cultivating his talent for speech by double majoring in Bible and Oral Interpretation. His double major turned a four year program into five, but he is still grateful for the choice.

During his sophomore year at BJU, Jerry met Beverly Jeanne Willis while working together to plan an Indiana state banquet for fellow Hoosiers. Beverly was from a small town in southern Indiana, and Jerry was instantly attracted to her sweet spirit, meekness, and country girl good looks. She was actually first to ask him on a date to a Sadie Hawkins event, but both were mutually interested in the other from the start. They were active during their college years as officers in Mission Prayer Band and student societies. Beverly graduated in 1965 with a degree in Elementary Education, and they were married that summer. During the following two years, Bev taught at a local public school to help put Jerry through school, and he graduated in 1967 with a Bachelor of Arts degree.

During his last year of undergraduate work, Jerry sought the Lord regarding what type of ministry to pursue. He was open to missions and the pastorate, but while listening to a message by an Army chaplain, he began to consider a career in the military chaplaincy. These were the last years of the Vietnam War, and Jerry caught a vision he couldn't escape for the lost

US servicemen dying in the jungles of Southeast Asia. In order to become an officer and a chaplain, Jerry needed a ministerial graduate degree, so he began pursuing the Master of Divinity at Bob Jones that fall during which time he also received his Army commission.

Jerry graduated with his MDiv in 1971 a few months after the birth of his first child, Kevin. That summer he attended chaplain school with the intent to ship out to Vietnam shortly after. However, the Nixon administration had begun to de-escalate the war and rather than receiving orders for deployment overseas, he was assigned to the inactive Army Reserve. Now with the need to locate work apart from the military, he approached the Director of Ministerial Training, Dr. Gilbert Stenholm, at BJU about ministry positions that might be available. Dr. Stenholm knew of a teaching position at Clearwater Christian College in Clearwater, FL, where his friend Dr. Arthur Steele presided; and Jerry was hired to teach starting that fall. Jerry taught various English Bible, Hermeneutics, Greek, and Church History courses and served part-time in the Dean of Students office, as well. It was during his time at Clearwater from 1971 to 1975 that he first became interested in Church History.

During the mid 1970s, Clearwater fell on hard times financially, and Jerry sent out his resume to a few other Christian colleges. Both Pillsbury Baptist Bible College in Owatonna, MN, and Piedmont Baptist College in Winston-Salem, NC, offered him a position. Piedmont won out, and Jerry moved his family, now including a daughter, Kara, to North Carolina to begin his role as Dean of Men and part-time Bible instructor for the fall of 1975. Jerry's interest in Church History only grew at Piedmont, and the more he taught, the less he enjoyed the Dean's office. It was during the late 1970s that Jerry rejoined the military as a chaplain for the North Carolina Army National Guard, where he was to enjoy a fruitful ministry for many years, retiring in 1999 with the rank of lieutenant-colonel.

In 1983 Jerry received permission from Piedmont to begin work on a PhD in Church History from Bob Jones University with a plan to teach full-time. After completing various pre-requisites at the University of North Carolina at Greensboro and Wake Forest University, he left the Dean's office and began coursework at BJU in 1986. During this time Piedmont began to face financial difficulties and was unable to meet payroll consistently, so Jerry volunteered for a chaplaincy program in Germany during the summers of 1986–88, to help pay the bills. During the fall of 1986 and 1987 he taught and volunteered for as much military service as possible, and during spring semesters he took resident courses at BJU to complete the PhD. In the spring of 1988, he attended a lengthy chaplaincy school and completed his dissertation. He remembers those years as some of the most challenging of his life.

During Jerry's thirteen years in North Carolina, he not only taught and counseled young people at Piedmont and ministered to hundreds of National Guardsmen, he also filled numerous pulpits in the region, serving at various times as interim pastor for two churches and senior pastor for one, the Northside Baptist Church of Winston-Salem. Jerry has always loved pulpit ministry, and his desire to preach was amply rewarded. It was also during his time at Piedmont that his Baptist convictions were solidified.

During his final years in North Carolina, Jerry became increasingly convinced that his days at Piedmont were coming to a close. Due to financial pressures and an increasing lack of fulfillment with extra responsibilities at Piedmont, he began to look for another ministry. In 1987 Dr. Rolland McCune, President of Detroit Baptist Theological Seminary in Allen Park, MI, visited Piedmont to recruit students. Jerry met him and a friendship ensued. McCune had mentioned that the current historical theology professor at DBTS was retiring, and both he and Jerry noted the providential nature of their meeting at this time. They corresponded during the following months, and eventually Dr. McCune extended an invitation to Jerry to chair the department of historical theology at DBTS starting in the fall of 1988, contingent upon completion of his PhD that spring. Jerry has been at DBTS ever since, teaching courses in historical theology, homiletics, and English Bible, as well as leading church history study tours to Europe.

The years at Detroit Baptist Theological Seminary have been fruitful for Jerry. In addition to frequent pulpit supply and continued ministry with the Army National Guard, his love of teaching has continued to grow as he has witnessed the propagation of his own ministry in the lives of his seminary students and student pastors in India, Africa, and the South Pacific. This principle of perpetuating oneself in ministry through a holistic approach to instruction in godly living and Christian character, which characterized the early American Puritans, drives Jerry, as well. The American Puritans have been a tremendous influence on him. Their concepts of legacy, perpetuation, and heritage loomed large for him and influenced not only his teaching, but also his family life and pulpit ministry. His greatest joy has been to witness his children and students follow the Lord in Christian service, thus perpetuating his own ministry in future generations.

If asked how he would like to be remembered, Jerry might reflect back on the life of one of his heroes—Amzi Clarence Dixon (1854–1925)—the subject of his doctoral dissertation. A. C. Dixon, a well-known early fundamentalist, was the epitome of a well-balanced, godly pastor who exhibited the very best of militant fundamentalism. He had a gentle soul and a compassionate spirit, but he was intolerant of apostasy and ungodliness. Dixon was a true defender of the faith; he took a strong stand for truth and was intolerant of compromise, but he never wavered in his genuine compassion for people. Another early fundamentalist, Dr. Bob Jones Sr., once said, "It's never right to do wrong to get a chance to do right." Jerry's children heard that quote many times from their father while growing up, and they witnessed, too, a life characterized by it. So, how might Jerry Priest choose to be remembered? Certainly, he would be pleased and honored by the way his children, grandchildren, and students remember him: as a man of conviction, like Dixon and Jones before him, willing to defend the truth at all costs, and as a humble man, faithful, gentle, and kind. In these he has never compromised.

2

Publications of Gerald L. Priest

Books

Baptist Family Catechism. Livonia, MI: N. W. Coughlin, 2003.
with Beverly Priest. *ABC Memory Verse Program*. Livonia, MI: N. W. Coughlin, 2003.

Chapters in Books

"Andrew Fuller, Hyper-Calvinism, and the 'Modern Question.'" In *'At the Pure Fountain of Thy Word': Andrew Fuller as an Apologist*, edited by Michael A. G. Haykin. Carlisle, Cumbria, UK: Paternoster, 2004.

"Abel Morgan, Sr." In *A Noble Company: Biographical Essays on Notable Particular-Regular Baptists in America*, edited by Terry Wolever. Vol. 1. Springfield, MO: Particular Baptist Press, 2006.

"Abel Morgan, Jr." In *A Noble Company: Biographical Essays on Notable Particular-Regular Baptists in America*, edited by Terry Wolever. Vol. 2. Springfield, MO: Particular Baptist Press, 2011.

"Peter Peterson Van Horne." *A Noble Company: Biographical Essays on Notable Particular-Regular Baptists in America*, edited by Terry Wolever. Vol. 3. Springfield, MO: Particular Baptist Press, 2013.

"Reune Runyon, Jr." *A Noble Company: Biographical Essays on Notable Particular-Regular Baptists in America*, edited by Terry Wolever. Vol. 4. Springfield, MO: Particular Baptist Press, 2014.

"David Irish." *A Noble Company: Biographical Essays on Notable Particular-Regular Baptists in America*, edited by Terry Wolever. Vol. 5. Springfield, MO: Particular Baptist Press, 2014.

"Lemuel Covell," "Asahel Morse," and "Lott Cary." *A Noble Company: Biographical Essays on Notable Particular-Regular Baptists in America*, edited by Terry Wolever. Vols. 6, 7, 8. Springfield, MO: Particular Baptist Press, forthcoming.

Publications of Gerald L. Priest

Contributions in *Biblical and Theological Essays: Selections from the Detroit Baptist Seminary Journal 1996–2000*, edited by William W. Combs. Winona Lake, IN: BMH, 2010.

Magazine and Journal Articles
(In Chronological Order)

"John Leland and the Bill of Rights." *Baptist Bulletin* 53 (February 1988) 13–14.
"Are Baptists Protestants." *FrontLine* (September-October 2002) 29, 32.
The following articles are from the *Detroit Baptist Seminary Journal*:
"A. C. Dixon, Chicago Liberals, and the Fundamentals." 1 (Spring 1996) 113–34.
"Revival and Revivalism: A Historical and Doctrinal Evaluation." 1 (Fall 1996) 223–52.
Review Article: "Justification By Faith Alone." 2 (Fall 1997) 127–34.
"William Jennings Bryan and the Scopes Trial: A Fundamentalist Perspective." 4 (Fall 1999) 51–83.
"Andrew Fuller's Response to the 'Modern Question'—A Reappraisal of *The Gospel Worthy of All Acceptation*." 6 (Fall 2001) 45–73.
"The Abel Morgans's Contribution to Baptist Ecclesiology in Colonial America." 8 (Fall 2003) 49–68.
"Early Fundamentalism's Legacy: What Is It and Will It Endure Through the 21st Century?" 9 (2004) 303–43.
"T. T. Shields the Fundamentalist: Man of Controversy." 10 (2005) 69–101.
"The Philadelphia Baptist Association and the Question of Authority." 12 (2007) 51–80.

3

"He Can Do It if He Will"

Jonathan Edwards, Inability, and the Theologians[1]

John Aloisi

IN HIS TREATISE ON the *Freedom of the Will* (1754), Jonathan Edwards (1703–58) set forward his answer to the question of how humankind can be genuinely responsible to please God and yet unable to do so apart from regenerating grace. Part of his solution to the problem of responsibility involved a distinction between natural and moral inability. Edwards argued that the unregenerate have a moral inability to please God, but he denied that they have a corresponding natural inability. Edwards was not the first theologian to propose this distinction, but he was one of the

---

1. It is a privilege and a pleasure for me to contribute to this volume in honor of my colleague and friend Dr. Gerald Priest. During the summer of 1998, I took a "test drive" course at Detroit Baptist Theological Seminary. I selected "History of Christian Doctrine" taught by Jerry Priest, and that experience sealed my decision to come to DBTS. Through that course and others he impressed upon me the importance of understanding the development of doctrine through the centuries. Since that summer he has also time and again proved a gracious and generous mentor. In light of his retirement this year, I have thought much about the fact that he is leaving behind very large shoes to fill. Blisters are inevitable, but he has done much to make the transition as comfortable as possible. This article, presented on the occasion of his retirement, discusses an issue that he has given much thought. We both hold Jonathan Edwards in the highest regard, but we also agree that his denial of natural inability was generally unwise.

first orthodox Calvinists to employ this concept in an extended argument against the Arminians.²

---

2. *Freedom of the Will* was published in 1754 around the midpoint of Edwards's ministry to the Indians in Stockbridge, Massachusetts, and just a few years before his death. Following A. A. Hodge, Gary Long asserted that the distinction between natural and moral inability was first made in 1618 by Scottish theologian John Cameron (c. 1579–1625) who taught at the theological school in Saumur, France. However, Sweeney has correctly pointed out that while Cameron "championed" the distinction and Moïse Amyraut (1596–1664) put the concept "on the theological map," neither Cameron nor Amyraut originated the distinction between natural and moral inability (Archibald Alexander Hodge, *Outlines of Theology* [reprint of 1879 ed., Grand Rapids: Zondervan, 1972] 341; Gary D. Long, "The Doctrine of Original Sin in New England Theology: From Jonathan Edwards to Edwards Amasa Park" [PhD diss., Dallas Theological Seminary, 1971] 18; Douglas A. Sweeney, *Nathaniel Taylor, New Haven Theology, and the Legacy of Jonathan Edwards* [New York: Oxford University Press, 2003] 74).

Fiering asserted that the distinction can be traced back at least to earlier Scholastic debates between Jesuits and Thomists over the concept of moral determination versus physical determination. But he claimed that Edwards most likely borrowed the idea from liberal Anglican Samuel Clarke (1675–1729) who had used the distinction to argue for a view quite different from that which Edwards defended. Sweeney has pointed out that "while Clarke surely represents one source of Edwards's knowledge of the natural/moral ability distinction, he is not the only source" (Norman Fiering, *Jonathan Edwards's Moral Thought and Its British Context* [Chapel Hill: University of North Carolina Press, 1981] 304; Samuel Clarke, *A Demonstration of the Being and Attributes of God and Other Writings*, ed. Ezio Vailati, Cambridge Texts in the History of Philosophy [Cambridge: Cambridge University Press, 1998] 21, 73; Sweeney, *Nathaniel Taylor, New Haven Theology, and the Legacy of Jonathan Edwards*, 202n19). In 1704 Clarke delivered a lecture titled "A Demonstration of the Being and Attributes of God." This lecture was published in 1705 as a book by the same title. It was widely circulated on both sides of the Atlantic and went through seven editions during Clarke's lifetime. Edwards cited this book along with several other titles by Clarke, but he never mentioned Clarke in connection with this distinction. Francis Turretin (1623–87) is another possible source where Edwards could have picked up the idea. Turretin discussed a distinction between natural and moral impotence in the first volume of his *Institutes* (pub. 1679). And interestingly, Edwards both recommended and lent his copy of Turretin's *Institutes* to Joseph Bellamy in 1747 the same year in which he first expressed to John Erskine his intention to write a treatise concerning, among other things, "Moral and Physical Inability" (Francis Turretin, *Institutes of Elenctic Theology*, trans. George Musgrave Giger, ed. James T. Dennison, Jr., 3 vols. [Phillipsburg, NJ: Presbyterian & Reformed, 1992–97] 1:675; Jonathan Edwards, *Letters and Personal Writings*, ed. George S. Claghorn, The Works of Jonathan Edwards [hereafter WJE], vol. 16 [New Haven: Yale University Press, 1998] 217; Jonathan Edwards, *The Freedom of the Will*, ed. Paul Ramsey, WJE, vol. 1 [New Haven: Yale University Press, 1957] 2; Jonathan Edwards, *Catalogues of Books*, ed. Peter J. Thuesen, WJE, vol. 26 [New Haven: Yale University Press, 2008] 350; Sereno Edwards Dwight, *The Life of President Edwards* [New York: G. & C. & H. Carvill, 1830] 250).

Once for All Delivered to the Saints

Toward the end of his essay on the will, Edwards sought to illustrate this distinction between natural and moral inability by means of a story about two men who had been imprisoned in a royal dungeon.[3] He described the first man as a criminal who had greatly offended his prince and had been thrown into prison as a just punishment for his crime. Eventually the king came to this man and commanded him to come forth from the prison. The king told the prisoner that if he would only leave his cell, humble himself before his sovereign, and beg for pardon he would be forgiven, set at liberty, and given great wealth. The man willingly repented of his crime against the prince and fully intended to accept the king's offer. But the king did not unlock the man's cell or release him from his iron bonds, and therefore the man was completely unable to obey the king's command despite his willingness. Edwards explained that this man who was willing to obey the king but was physically prevented from doing so was subject to natural inability.

Edwards then described the second prisoner as a haughty and unreasonable man who harbored a treasonous spirit. This man was an inveterate enemy of the king who for his rebellion had long been locked up in heavy chains and kept in miserable circumstances. At length the gracious prince came to this man's cell, unlocked the door, and released him from his chains. The prince then told the man that if he would only step forth from his cell, acknowledge his rebellion, and humble himself he would be forgiven, set at liberty, and given great wealth. But this prisoner was so haughty and filled with malice toward the prince that he was unwilling to accept the prince's kind offer. In this case, the problem lay not in the man's physical ability but rather in his will. He possessed the natural ability to fulfill the conditions for forgiveness, but he was not inclined to exercise that ability. This man's condition, Edwards noted, was completely different from the first man's. While the first prisoner was subject to a natural inability to obey the king's command, the second prisoner possessed the natural ability but was subject to a moral inability to obey because this prisoner could "easily do it if he pleases."[4]

For many readers this illustration made Edwards's distinction between natural and moral inability much easier to understand. However, if it

---

3. Edwards, *Freedom of the Will*, 362–63. This illustration appears in the context of Edwards's discussion of natural and moral necessity. However, his distinction with regard to necessity is parallel to his distinction between natural and moral inability, and Edwards clearly intended to illustrate the two types of inability.

4. Edwards, *Freedom of the Will*, 363.

elucidated what Edwards meant by natural inability and moral inability, it did not cause all his readers to accept the distinction much less his overall argument. As Edwards anticipated, his treatise on the will met with a mixed response.[5] One historian noted, "Whatever else its publication may have done, it produced a state of incredible intellectual confusion."[6] Arminians were generally convinced that Edwards was wrong in his conclusions, but they had a difficult time deciding which part of his argument to attack.[7] A number of the Edwardseans on the other hand, misunderstood Edwards or took his ideas far beyond his original intent.[8]

As a result of Edwards's arguments in the *Freedom of the Will*, many of his followers ultimately embraced his distinction between natural and moral inability. E. Brooks Holifield has correctly noted that this distinction became "one of the hallmarks of the Edwardsean tradition."[9] Some of Edwards's followers emphasized this distinction more than Edwards ever did, and this caused a number of later Calvinists to look askance at his *Freedom of the Will*.[10] However, other Calvinists adopted the distinction and put it to

---

5. In 1762, an anonymous and wholly negative review from a generally Arminian perspective appeared in the *Monthly Review*. Shortly thereafter, Calvinist James Dana (1735–1812) penned two of the earliest extended critiques of *Freedom of the Will* in 1770 and 1773. Arguing against Dana's 1770 work, Stephen West (1735–1819) provided an early Calvinistic defense of Edwards's treatise. And from an Arminian position, Samuel West (1730–1807) wrote two short books critiquing *Freedom of the Will* near the close of the century which were then rebutted by Jonathan Edwards the younger (review of *Freedom of the Will*, by Jonathan Edwards, *Monthly Review* 27 [December 1762] 434–38; James Dana, *An Examination of the Late Reverend President Edwards's "Enquiry on Freedom of Will"* [Boston: Daniel Kneeland, 1770]; James Dana, *The "Examination of the Late Rev'd President Edwards's Enquiry on Freedom of Will," Continued* [New Haven: Thomas & Samuel Green, 1773]; Stephen West, *An Essay on Moral Agency* [New Haven: Thomas & Samuel Green, 1772]; Samuel West, *Essays on Liberty and Necessity* [Boston: Samuel Hall, 1793], Samuel West, *Essays on Liberty and Necessity*, Part Second [New Bedford, MA: John Spooner, 1795]; Jonathan Edwards [the younger], *A Dissertation Concerning Liberty and Necessity; Containing Remarks on the Essays of Dr. Samuel West* [Worchester, MA: Leonard Worchester, 1797]).

6. Conrad Wright, "Edwards and the Arminians on the Freedom of the Will," *Harvard Theological Review* 35 (1942) 241.

7. Wright, "Edwards and the Arminians on the Freedom of the Will," 251.

8. Wright, "Edwards and the Arminians on the Freedom of the Will," 241.

9. E. Brooks Holifield, *Theology in America: Christian Thought from the Age of the Puritans to the Civil War* (New Haven: Yale University Press, 2003) 122. See also, Douglas A. Sweeney and Allen C. Guelzo, eds., *The New England Theology: From Jonathan Edwards to Edwards Amasa Park* (Grand Rapids: Baker, 2006) 57.

10. Holifield, *Theology in America*, 122.

various uses. Andrew Fuller (1754–1815), for example, employed it in his *Gospel Worthy of All Acceptation* (1786), a book which provided much of the theological foundation for the modern missions movement.[11]

Since the time of Edwards, his distinction between natural and moral inability has been embraced by some theologians and opposed by others. This article will examine the main criticisms which have been lodged against Edwards's view by those who shared much of his Calvinistic theology. It will argue that several of the criticisms of Edwards's distinction between natural and moral inability have pointed out genuine weaknesses in his view. Therefore, although Edwards's distinction has been accepted by many theologians, there is good reason to question its merit.

Edwards's writings have often been subject to misunderstanding. His characteristically abstract arguments are often challenging and sometimes quite prone to misinterpretation. Therefore, before looking at criticisms of Edwards's theory which have been proposed by other writers, it will be helpful to briefly examine Edwards's own explanation of the distinction between natural and moral inability.

Jonathan Edwards's Distinction between Natural and Moral Inability

Edwards began the *Freedom of the Will* by defining terms and phrases relevant to his argument, and in fact he devoted considerable space to this effort. Correctly understanding Edwards's terminology is an essential part of properly understanding his argument because sometimes Edwards intended a very specific but not readily apparent meaning when he used certain terms.

---

11. Andrew Fuller, *The Complete Works of the Rev. Andrew Fuller: With a Memoir of His Life, by Andrew Gunton Fuller*, 3 vols., reprint of 3rd London ed.; rev., with additions, by Joseph Belcher (Harrison, VA: Sprinkle, 1988) 2:376–78. The first edition of Fuller's *Gospel Worthy of All Acceptation* was published in 1786; a second edition followed in 1801. For helpful discussions of the influence of Edwards on Fuller see, Gerald L. Priest, "Andrew Fuller, Hyper-Calvinism, and the 'Modern Question,'" in *"At the Pure Fountain of Thy Word": Andrew Fuller as an Apologist*, ed. Michael A. G. Haykin, Studies in Baptist History and Thought, vol. 6 (Carlisle, Cumbria, UK: Paternoster, 2004) 58–72; Gerald L. Priest, "Andrew Fuller's Response to the 'Modern Question'—A Reappraisal of *The Gospel Worthy of All Acceptation*," *Detroit Baptist Seminary Journal* 6 (Fall 2001) 45–73; Thomas J. Nettles, "The Influence of Jonathan Edwards on Andrew Fuller," *Eusebeia* 9 (Spring 2008) 97–116; Chris Chun, "A Mainspring of Missionary Thought: Andrew Fuller on 'Natural and Moral Inability,'" *American Baptist Quarterly* 25 (Winter 2006) 335–55.

In the opening pages of his book, Edwards defined the will as "that by which the mind chooses anything."[12] Expanding this definition, he explained that "the faculty of the will is that faculty or power or principle of mind by which it is capable of choosing: an act of the will is the same as an act of choosing or choice."[13] By this Edwards did not mean to imply that the will is the agent which actually does the choosing. Rather he meant that the will is the power or the means by which the mind chooses anything.[14] In other words, the mind governs the will and determines its course. Edwards believed that every act of the will involves the mind choosing one thing over another and that this choosing is always in conformity with the person's desires. He pointed out that "a man never, in any instance, wills anything contrary to his desires, or desires anything contrary to his will."[15] Therefore when people exercise their wills, they always do so in keeping with their desires.

Along this line Edwards argued that the will is always determined by something outside itself. He wrote, "To talk of the determination of the will, supposes an effect, which must have a cause. If the will be determined, there is a determiner."[16] The will's decisions are never uncaused, but neither are they self-determined. Edwards explained, "it is that motive, which, as it stands in the view of the mind, is the strongest, that determines the will."[17] Therefore, the will is always determined by what the mind perceives to be the strongest motive. One of Edwards's main objectives in discussing the determination of the will was to disprove the Arminian theory of a self-determined will. As he saw it, a self-determined will is a logical impossibility.

Edwards defined the term *motive* as "the whole of that which moves, excites or invites the mind to volition, whether that be one thing singly, or many things conjunctly."[18] He noted that numerous things may work

---

12. Edwards, *Freedom of the Will*, 137. Pages 1–128 of this edition contain an introduction by the editor.

13. Edwards, *Freedom of the Will*, 137. Elsewhere Edwards described the will as "the mind's inclination with respect to its own immediate actions" (Jonathan Edwards, *Scientific and Philosophical Writings*, ed. Wallace E. Anderson, WJE, vol. 6 [New Haven: Yale University Press, 1980] 376).

14. C. Samuel Storms, *Tragedy in Eden: Original Sin in the Theology of Jonathan Edwards* (Lanham, MD: University Press of America, 1985) 157.

15. Edwards, *Freedom of the Will*, 139.

16. Edwards, *Freedom of the Will*, 141.

17. Edwards, *Freedom of the Will*, 141.

18. Edwards, *Freedom of the Will*, 141.

together to produce a single complex motive. When considering the strength of a motive, Edwards held that the strongest motive is that which produces a "particular act of volition, whether that be the strength of one thing alone, or of many together."[19] So regardless of whether a motive was simple or complex, he viewed the motive in terms of its ability to effect a volitional act.

The philosophical concept of necessity is also fundamental to Edwards's argument. He wrote,

> The word "necessary," as used in common speech, is a relative term; and relates to some supposed opposition made to the existence of the thing spoken of, which is overcome, or proves in vain to hinder or alter it. That is necessary, in the original and proper sense of the word, which is, or will be, notwithstanding all supposable opposition. To say, that a thing is necessary, is the same thing as to say, that it is impossible [it] should not be.[20]

Edwards believed that this common way of speaking about necessity is valid, but he wanted to distinguish the way he intended to use the term from its common, relative sense. He pointed out that "these terms 'necessary,' 'impossible,' etc. are often used by philosophers and metaphysicians in a sense quite diverse from their common use and original signification: for they apply them to many cases in which no opposition is supposed or supposable."[21] When Edwards spoke of necessity, he meant philosophical necessity which "is really nothing else than the full and fixed connection between the things signified by the subject and predicate of a proposition, which affirms something to be true."[22] It was this type of necessity which Edwards wanted to prove is not inconsistent with genuine liberty.[23]

Edwards's discussion of philosophical necessity was intended to be a backdrop for his explanation of natural and moral necessity and the related question of natural and moral inability. He defined moral necessity as "that necessity of connection and consequence, which arises from such *moral causes*, as the strength of inclination, or motives, and the connection which there is in many cases between these, and such certain volitions

---

19. Edwards, *Freedom of the Will*, 141.
20. Edwards, *Freedom of the Will*, 149.
21. Edwards, *Freedom of the Will*, 151.
22. Edwards, *Freedom of the Will*, 152.
23. Edwards, *Freedom of the Will*, 152.

and actions."[24] In other words, moral necessity involves a definite connection between moral causes and specific acts of the will. In distinction from this Edwards wrote, "By 'natural necessity,' as applied to men, I mean such necessity as men are under through the force of natural causes; as distinguished from what are called moral causes, such as habits and dispositions of the heart, and moral motives and inducements."[25] In Edwards's understanding, while moral necessity arises from moral causes, natural necessity arises from strictly natural causes outside the will.

Concerning these two types of necessity, Edwards asserted, "moral necessity may be as absolute, as natural necessity. That is, the effect may be as perfectly connected with its moral cause, as a naturally necessary effect is with its natural cause."[26] Edwards believed that moral necessity involves genuine philosophical necessity. Moral necessity does not mean that the agent will merely face great opposition which will tend to prevent a different volitional act; instead it involves the agent's absolute inability to perform any other volitional act.

Edwards's understanding of natural and moral necessity is closely tied to his concept of natural and moral inability. This is the case because necessity always involves a corresponding inability to do otherwise.[27] Concerning natural inability, Edwards wrote, "We are said to be *naturally* unable to do a thing, when we can't do it if we will, because what is most commonly called nature don't [sic] allow it, or because of some impeding defect or obstacle that is extrinsic to the will; either in the faculty of understanding, constitution of body, or external objects."[28] As Edwards understood it, natural inability involves a thing being impossible for a person to perform because of something other than the person's will.

Edwards distinguished between two types of moral inability, that which is "general and habitual" and that which is "particular and occasional." He defined general and habitual inability as "an inability in the heart to all exercises or acts of will of that nature or kind, through a fixed and habitual inclination, or an habitual and stated defect, or want of a

---

24. Edwards, *Freedom of the Will*, 156.
25. Edwards, *Freedom of the Will*, 156–57.
26. Edwards, *Freedom of the Will*, 157.
27. Allen C. Guelzo, *Edwards on the Will: A Century of American Theological Debate* (Middletown, CT: Wesleyan University Press, 1989) 47–48.
28. Edwards, *Freedom of the Will*, 159.

certain kind of inclination."[29] General and habitual inability relates to certain types of acts rather than to specific acts themselves. In contrast to this, Edwards viewed particular and occasional inability as "an inability of the will or heart to a particular act, through the strength or defect of present motives, or of inducements presented to the view of the understanding, on this occasion."[30] This type of inability concerns specific acts of the will as they are influenced by present motives. Throughout the treatise, when Edwards speaks of moral inability, it is usually the general and habitual sense which he intends.

Edwards used the term *moral inability* quite often, but he admitted that moral inability alone is not properly called inability.[31] He explained, "a man has a thing in his power, if he has it in his choice, or at his election: and a man can't be truly said to be unable to do a thing, when he can do it if he will."[32] Edwards held that moral inability consists solely in disinclination or, to phrase it another way, it consists in "the opposition or want of inclination."[33] In such a condition the person's will is not willing to do the thing commanded, though he could do it if he so desired. This type of inability, Edwards argued "never renders anything improperly the subject matter of precept or command, and never can excuse any person in disobedience, or want of conformity to a command."[34] In other words, he held that moral inability provides no basis for excuse. And therefore against the Arminians he argued that human responsibility is fully compatible with moral inability.

On the other hand, Edwards asserted that "natural inability, arising from the want of natural capacity, or external hindrance (which alone is properly called inability) without doubt wholly excuses, or makes a thing improperly the matter of command."[35] He further explained this idea: "If

---

29. Edwards, *Freedom of the Will*, 160.
30. Edwards, *Freedom of the Will*, 160.
31. Edwards, *Freedom of the Will*, 161–62, 308–9.
32. Edwards, *Freedom of the Will*, 162.

33 Edwards, *Freedom of the Will*, 159. He similarly stated that "a man may then be said to be morally unable to do a thing, when he is under the influence or prevalence of a contrary inclination, or has a want of inclination, under such circumstances and views" (*Freedom of the Will*, 305).

34. Edwards, *Freedom of the Will*, 309.

35. Edwards, *Freedom of the Will*, 309. Edwards also noted, "all inability that excuses, may be resolved into one thing; namely, want of natural capacity or strength; either capacity of understanding, or external strength" (*Freedom of the Will*, 310).

men are excused from doing or acting any good thing, supposed to be commanded, it must be through some defect or obstacle that is not in the will itself, but extrinsic to it; either in the capacity of understanding, or body, or outward circumstances."[36] This means that if people lack the natural capacity to obey a divine command or are hindered by something outside their wills, they are not accountable for their failure to comply. As Edwards stated it such a natural inability "without doubt wholly excuses" the person from any responsibility to obey the command regardless of who issued it.

Having laid out his distinction between natural and moral inability, Edwards declared, "So that all this grand objection of Arminians against the inability of fallen men to exert faith in Christ, or to perform other spiritual gospel duties, from the sincerity of God's counsels and invitations, must be without force."[37] Edwards believed that his distinction between natural and moral inability explained how humans could be both unable to exercise faith in Christ and yet wholly responsible for their unbelief. He believed that by denying natural inability he had established the basis of human responsibility. Arminians, however, have generally not been convinced that Edwards's explanation resolved the tension.[38] And as will be seen, a number of Calvinists have also raised questions about the validity of Edwards's distinction between natural and moral inability.[39]

Objections to Jonathan Edwards's Distinction

The discussion that follows will examine four types of objections raised by Calvinists against Edwards's distinction between natural and moral inability and his corresponding denial of natural inability. Although other

---

36. Edwards, *Freedom of the Will*, 309.

37. Edwards, *Freedom of the Will*, 311.

38. Major Arminian (or non-Calvinistic) responses include Albert Taylor Bledsoe, *An Examination of President Edwards's Inquiry into the Freedom of the Will* (Philadelphia: H. Hooker, 1845); Rowland G. Hazard, *Freedom of the Mind in Willing* (New York: D. Appleton & Co., 1864); D. D. Whedon, *The Freedom of the Will as a Basis of Human Responsibility and Divine Government* (New York: Carlton & Porter, 1864).

39. In addition to James Dana (mentioned above) and the theologians discussed below, several early nineteenth-century Calvinists wrote extended critiques of Edwards's book. These include Henry Philip Tappan, *A Review of Edwards's "Inquiry into the Freedom of the Will"* (New York: John S. Taylor, 1839); Henry Philip Tappan, *The Doctrine of the Will, Determined by an Appeal to Consciousness* (New York: Wiley & Putnam, 1840); Jeremiah Day, *An Examination of President Edwards's Inquiry on the Freedom of the Will* (New Haven, CT: Durrie & Peck, 1841).

criticisms have been lodged against Edwards's view, the difficulties raised can largely be reduced to these four main issues.

The Problem of Terminology

Archibald Alexander Hodge (1823–86) is not usually numbered among Edwards's critics. And indeed with regard to the issue of natural and moral inability, Hodge stated that he recognized the distinction as valid in the sense that Edwards held and used it.[40] Nevertheless, Hodge offered five reasons why he seriously objected to Edwards's phraseology.[41] His reasons are not equally compelling, but together they comprise a substantial argument for rejecting the terminology used by Edwards.

First, Hodge noted that the terms used by Edwards have no warrant in Scripture.[42] Hodge pointed out that the Bible never states that humans have one type of ability to obey God but not another.[43] Instead, the consistent testimony of Scripture is that the unregenerate are wholly unable to please God.[44] Since Scripture describes humanity as completely unable, Hodge thought it unwise to speak about sinners possessing some type of ability.

Second, Hodge claimed that the terminology used by Edwards "has never been adopted in the Creed Statements of any one of the Reformed Churches."[45] Hodge believed that Edwards's language lacked historical precedent or creedal acceptance and was therefore suspect.[46] Although not

---

40. Hodge, *Outlines of Theology*, 341.

41. Hodge, *Outlines of Theology*, 341–42.

42. Hodge, *Outlines of Theology*, 341. For this reason among others, Berkhof rejected the distinction altogether (Louis Berkhof, *Systematic Theology*, 4th revised and enlarged ed. [Grand Rapids: Eerdmans, 1996] 247–48).

43. Although Edwards never directly stated in *Freedom of the Will* that fallen humanity possesses the natural ability to obey and please God, this was a clear implication of his denial of natural inability. The concept of natural ability which Edwards implied in *Freedom of the Will* was picked up by many of his followers and in fact became a major theme of their theology and preaching (William G. T. Shedd, *Dogmatic Theology*, 2nd ed., 3 vols. (Nashville: Thomas Nelson, 1980) 2:221; Priest, "Andrew Fuller, Hyper-Calvinism, and the 'Modern Question,'" 60n60; Sweeney and Guelzo, eds., *New England Theology*, 57–58).

44. Hodge, *Outlines of Theology*, 341.

45. Hodge, *Outlines of Theology*, 341.

46. The aversion of the Hodges to theological innovation is well known. Recall, for example, Charles Hodge's assertion that "a new idea never originated in this Seminary [Princeton]" (Archibald Alexander Hodge, *The Life of Charles Hodge* [New York: Charles

mentioned by Hodge, the terms used by Edwards had been specifically rejected in the Helvetic Formula Consensus (1675). Canons twenty-one and twenty-two of that document state, "This inability may indeed be called moral in so far as it pertains to a moral subject or object: but it ought to be at the same time called natural.... We hold therefore that they speak inaccurately and dangerously, who call this inability to believe moral inability, and do not say that it is natural."[47] Similarly, Francis Turretin (1623–87) wrote, "Nor do they make a better escape who pretend this impotence to be moral, not natural; and thus a thing not absolutely and simply impossible to man, but that man can do it if he wishes. We answer that whether this impotence be called natural or moral . . . it is certainly inextricable to man."[48] Edwards's use of this distinction in order to deny natural inability not only lacked precedent within the Calvinist tradition, it was also contrary to what many orthodox Calvinists had taught.

Hodge's third objection flowed from his belief that the terminology employed in the distinction "is essentially ambiguous."[49] Hodge explained,

> It has been often used to express, sometimes to cover, Semipelagian error. It is naturally misleading and confusing when addressed to the struggling sinner. This language assures him that he is able in a certain sense, when it is only true that he possesses *some* of the essential prerequisites of ability. Ability *begins* only after *all* its essential conditions are present.... It is simply untrue and misleading to tell him he has natural *ability*, when the fact is precisely that he is unable.[50]

Scribner's Sons, 1880] 521).

47. Martin I. Klauber, "The Helvetic Formula Consensus (1675): An Introduction and Translation," *Trinity Journal* 11 (Spring 1990) 122. Admittedly, John Henry Heidegger, Francis Turretin, and Lucas Gernler wrote these words in opposition to the Amyraldianism of the Saumur school. However, the point stands that the Swiss Reformed theologians rejected the exact terminology that Edwards later adopted. And somewhat tellingly, Edwards was later noted as having brought the theology of Saumur to prominence in America (Charles Augustus Briggs, *Theological Symbolics* [New York: Charles Scribner's Sons, 1914] 374).

48. Turretin, *Institutes of Elenctic Theology*, 1:675.

49. Hodge, *Outlines of Theology*, 341. Robert Dabney wrote, "This pair of terms is utterly ambiguous and inappropriate.... I never employ them" (Robert L. Dabney, *Lectures in Systematic Theology* [reprint ed., Grand Rapids: Zondervan, 1972] 597). Note the similar comments by Louis Berkhof and Charles Hodge (Berkhof, *Systematic Theology*, 248; Charles Hodge, *Systematic Theology*, 3 vols. [reprint ed., Grand Rapids: Eerdmans, 1993] 2:265).

50. Hodge, *Outlines of Theology*, 341.

Hodge recognized that the terms used by Edwards could easily be employed to express doctrinal error, and in fact, he knew that this had often been the case. Moreover, Hodge thought that Edwards's posited natural ability should not be regarded as ability because it does not entail the actual ability to accomplish the thing in view.

Fourth, Hodge asserted that the word *natural* is not the proper antithesis of the word *moral*. This is true, he said, in part because "a thing may be at the same time natural and moral."[51] In fact, he said this is precisely the case with regard to inability because fallen humanity's inability while certainly moral is also natural. Therefore, the two terms should not be set in opposition to each other. A number of other Calvinists have voiced similar objections to Edwards's strong distinction between the words *natural* and *moral*.[52]

The fifth reason Hodge suggested for objecting to Edwards's terminology was that "the language does not accurately express the important distinction intended."[53] He explained, "The inability is moral and is not either physical or constitutional. It has its ground not in the want of any faculty, but in the corrupt moral state of the faculties."[54] In other words, Hodge believed that the terms used by Edwards clouded the nature of human inability because they seemed to ignore the moral condition of man's faculties. Hodge agreed with Edwards that fallen man possesses the faculties prerequisite to genuine ability, but Hodge believed Edwards was mistaken in describing these faculties apart from their moral condition which inevitably prevents them from being exercised aright.

In summary, Hodge did not argue that Edwards's distinction was completely invalid as long as it was used exactly as Edwards meant it. However, Hodge thought that Edwards's terminology should be abandoned because of the absence of biblical or historical precedent to support it and because of its fundamental lack of precision.

---

51. Hodge, *Outlines of Theology*, 342.

52. Hodge, *Systematic Theology*, 2:265; Augustus Hopkins Strong, *Systematic Theology*, 3 vols. in 1 (Valley Forge, PA: Judson, 1907) 640; Berkhof, *Systematic Theology*, 248. Although A. A. Hodge was the son of Charles Hodge, his *Outlines of Theology* (1860) was published before his father's *Systematic Theology* (1871–73).

53. Hodge, *Outlines of Theology*, 342.

54. Hodge, *Outlines of Theology*, 342. See also, Berkhof, *Systematic Theology*, 248; Strong, *Systematic Theology*, 640.

The Effects of Depravity

No one who has read Edwards's book *Original Sin* (1758) doubts that he believed in the doctrine of total depravity. Throughout that book and elsewhere, Edwards declared that humanity is utterly depraved and wholly dependent on the grace of God for salvation. And yet, Edwards's denial of natural inability combined with his assertion that moral inability alone is not properly called inability could be interpreted as an implicit denial of total inability.[55] In other words, Edwards held that the only inability which sinners possess is moral inability, and as he put it, "no inability whatsoever which is merely moral, is properly called by the name of 'inability.'"[56] He also wrote, "the word 'inability' is used in a sense very diverse from its original import. The word signifies only a natural inability, in the proper use of it."[57] So this raises the question, if an unregenerate person is not subject to natural inability and if that individual's moral inability is not properly called inability, is that person really subject to what is usually termed total inability? At best Edwards lacked clarity on this point, and his equivocation did nothing to aid his real purpose. As Herman Bavinck put it rather bluntly, "by [Edwards'] refusal to call this disinclination toward the good 'natural impotence,' he fostered a lot of misunderstanding and actually aided the cause of Pelagianism."[58]

Similarly Edwards's belief that nothing in the mind or power of sinners prevents them from fulfilling their spiritual duties seems to imply some type of partial depravity or perhaps a disconnect between depravity and inability.[59] By denying natural inability Edwards appears to have suggested

---

55. Edwards, *Freedom of the Will*, 308–9.

56. Edwards, *Freedom of the Will*, 308. Charles Hodge agreed with Edwards that disinclination or lack of will alone does not constitute inability (*Systematic Theology*, 2:265). And more recently, William Breitenbach pointed out that Edwards's moral inability "is a 'cannot' that is really a powerful 'will not.' Indeed, technically speaking, it is not even an inability; it is an unwillingness or disinclination" ("Piety *and* Moralism: Edwards and the New Divinity," in *Jonathan Edwards and the American Experience*, ed. Nathan O. Hatch and Harry S. Stout [New York: Oxford University Press, 1988] 187).

57. Edwards, *Freedom of the Will*, 161.

58. Herman Bavinck, *Reformed Dogmatics*, trans. John Vriend, ed. John Bolt, 4 vols. (Grand Rapids: Baker, 2003–2008) 3:122.

59. Priest, "Andrew Fuller, Hyper-Calvinism, and the 'Modern Question,'" 61. E.g., Edwards stated, "To ascribe a nonperformance to the want of power or ability, is not just; because the thing wanting is not a being *able*, but a being *willing*" (*Freedom of the Will*, 162).

that some parts of the human constitution have not been corrupted by the fall. In his *Religious Affections* (1746), Edwards described the human soul as possessing two faculties, namely understanding and will. The understanding he identified as the faculty of perception and speculation. This faculty is the means by which humans exercise discernment and judgment. The will, on the other hand, he recognized as the source of determination or inclination. Edwards also called this faculty the mind or the heart of man.[60] Some twenty years before he wrote *Freedom of the Will*, Edwards described sinners as depraved in all of their faculties. He declared, "They are totally corrupt, in every part, in all their faculties; and all the principles of their nature, their understandings, and wills; and in all their dispositions and affections, their heads, their hearts, are totally depraved."[61] But in *Freedom of the Will*, Edwards described human inability as tied exclusively to the will. He said that failure to obey a command due to "some defect or obstacle that is not in the will itself" is a natural inability which "without doubt wholly excuses."[62] And therefore, any inability due to capacity of understanding or strength removes culpability.[63] However, tying inability exclusively to the will seems to contradict several passages of Scripture which depict man's understanding as fallen, for any faculty of man which is depraved cannot rightly be spoken of as possessing spiritual ability. While Paul clearly viewed sinners as unwilling to repent apart from divine grace, he also described the mind and heart of sinners as totally depraved and therefore completely unable to please God. In his letter to the Ephesians, Paul wrote, "You must no longer walk as the Gentiles do, in the futility of their minds. They are darkened in their understanding, alienated from the life of God because of the

---

60. Edwards wrote, "God has indued the soul with two faculties: one is that by which it is capable of perception and speculation, or by which it discerns and views and judges of things; which is called understanding. The other faculty is that by which the soul does not merely perceive and view things, but is some way inclined with respect to the things it views or considers.... This faculty is called by various names: it is sometimes called the *inclination*: and, as it has respect to the actions that are determined and governed by it, is called the *will*: and the *mind*, with regard to the exercises of this faculty, is often called the *heart*" (Jonathan Edwards, *Religious Affections*, ed. John E. Smith, WJE, vol. 2 [New Haven: Yale University Press, 1959] 96).

61. Jonathan Edwards, "The Justice of God in the Damnation of Sinners," (sermon preached c. May 1735) in *Sermons and Discourses 1734–38*, ed. M. X. Lesser, WJE, vol. 19 (New Haven: Yale University Press, 2001) 344.

62. Edwards, *Freedom of the Will*, 309.

63. Edwards, *Freedom of the Will*, 309–10.

ignorance that is in them, due to their hardness of heart" (Eph 4:17–18).[64] Here Paul used the same words later adopted by Edwards, but in contrast to Edwards's denial of natural inability, Paul described the unbeliever's mind, understanding, and heart as futile, darkened, and hardened.

In addition to this tension with Scripture, Edwards also placed himself in conflict with what many Calvinists had traditionally affirmed about the effects of depravity. For example, the *Westminster Confession of Faith* (1647) stated, "By this sin [Adam and Eve] fell from their original righteousness and communion with God, and so became dead in sin, and *wholly defiled in all the faculties and parts of soul and body*. . . . From this original corruption, whereby we are utterly indisposed, disabled, and made opposite to all good, and wholly inclined to all evil, do proceed all actual transgressions.[65] Such a description of the effects of the fall on "all the faculties and parts of soul and body" seems to imply a depravity and hence an inability which exists beyond the will alone.

Although Edwards did not actually teach partial depravity, his lack of clarity on this subject left the door open for the New Divinity theologians and the Taylorites after him.[66] In contrast to Edwards's ambiguity, A. H. Strong (1836–1921), stated,

> We hold, therefore, to an inability which is both natural and moral,—moral, as having its source in the self-corruption of man's moral nature and the fundamental aversion of his will to God;—natural, as being inborn, and as affecting with partial paralysis all his natural powers of intellect, affection, conscience, and will. For his inability, in both these aspects of it, man is responsible.[67]

More recently, but with similar language, Robert Reymond described humanity's fallen condition when he wrote,

> Man in his raw, natural state as he comes from the womb is *morally and spiritually corrupt in disposition and character*. Every part of his being—his mind, his will, his emotions, his affections, his conscience, his body—has been affected by sin (this is what is meant by the doctrine of *total* depravity). His understanding is

---

64. Unless otherwise noted, all Scriptural citations are from the ESV (2001). See also passages such as John 12:40; Rom 1:21, 28; 8:6–7; Col 1:21.

65. *Westminster Confession of Faith*, 6.2, 4 (emphasis added).

66. Sweeney, *Nathaniel Taylor, New Haven Theology, and the Legacy of Jonathan Edwards*, 32, 73–83.

67. Strong, *Systematic Theology*, 640.

> darkened, his mind is at enmity with God, his will to act is slave to his darkened understanding and rebellious mind, his heart is corrupt, his emotions are perverted, his affections naturally gravitate to that which is evil and ungodly, his conscience is untrustworthy, and his body is subject to mortality.[68]

Edwards's denial of natural inability implied that some parts of the human constitution have not been directly affected by the fall. This denial appears to have been a departure from Scripture and also from what Calvinists have traditionally taught about the extent of the effects of human depravity.[69]

The Nature of Moral Inability

As mentioned above, Edwards's understanding of natural and moral inability is logically related to his view of natural and moral necessity. It has also been noted that Edwards denied that moral inability alone constitutes what is properly called inability.[70] But herein lies a problem with Edwards's explanation of moral inability. If moral necessity is properly called necessity, then moral inability is properly called inability because moral necessity always involves a corresponding inability to do otherwise. And this corresponding inability must be as absolute as the moral necessity to which it is related. Edwards readily admitted that "moral necessity may be as absolute, as natural necessity."[71] But he did not hold that moral inability is as absolute as natural inability. As William G. T. Shedd (1820–94), correctly pointed out,

> Edwards is inconsistent in denying that moral inability is properly called *inability*. For the sinner's moral necessity of sinning is the very same thing as his moral inability to obedience. If, therefore, Edwards was willing to say that moral necessity is as real and

---

68. Robert L. Reymond, *A New Systematic Theology of the Christian Faith* (Nashville: Thomas Nelson, 1998) 450.

69. Comparing Edwards to Dabney, Thomas C. Johnson noted that Edwards "changed . . . somewhat, the theological system which he wished to defend" ("Robert Lewis Dabney—A Sketch," in *In Memoriam: Robert Lewis Dabney*, ed. Charles William Dabney [Knoxville: University of Tennessee Press, 1899] 8–9).

70. Edwards, *Freedom of the Will*, 161–62, 308–9.

71. Edwards, *Freedom of the Will*, 157.

absolute as natural necessity, he should have been willing to say that moral inability is as real and absolute as natural inability.[72]

Part of the reason why Edwards avoided describing moral inability as absolute inability probably stemmed from his desire to answer the Arminian charge that complete inability is inconsistent with moral obligation. But in failing to describe moral inability in absolute terms, Edwards appears to have conceded an essential point to the Arminians and in doing so to have departed from his Calvinistic forebears as well.[73] As Charles Hodge later wrote, "Augustinians have ever taught that this inability is absolute and entire. It is natural as well as moral. It is as complete, although of a different kind, as the inability of the blind to see, of the deaf to hear, or of the dead to restore themselves to life."[74] And as Wright points out, "The fact that Edwards was apparently departing from the accepted Calvinist doctrine was not lost on the Arminians."[75]

The Question of Natural Ability

By his denial of natural inability, Edwards implied that all humans possess the natural ability to repent of their sins and believe the gospel. All that the ungodly are lacking, he argued, is the inclination to do so. As he put it, "the thing wanting is not a being *able*, but a being *willing*. There are faculties of mind, and capacity of nature, and everything else, sufficient, but a disposition: nothing is wanting but a will."[76]

---

72. Shedd, *Dogmatic Theology*, 2:230.

73. Shedd, *Dogmatic Theology*, 2:231, 242–45. Reymond responded quite differently than Edwards to the Arminian claim that total inability is inconsistent with responsibility to obey God's commands. Reymond asserted that "God deals with man according to his *obligation*, not according to the measure of his ability. Before the Fall, man had both the obligation and the ability to obey God. As a result of the Fall, he retained the former but lost the latter. Man's inability to obey, arising from the corruption of his nature, does not remove from him his obligation to love God with all his heart, soul, mind, and strength, and his neighbor as himself. His obligation to obey God remains intact. If God dealt with man today according to his ability to obey, he would have to reduce his moral demands to the vanishing point. Conversely, if we determined the measure of man's ability from the sweeping obligations implicit in the divine commands, then we would need to predicate *total ability* for man" (Reymond, *A New Systematic Theology*, 454).

74. Hodge, *Systematic Theology*, 2:267.

75. Wright, "Edwards and the Arminians on the Freedom of the Will," 242.

76. Edwards, *Freedom of the Will*, 162.

Edwards affirmed that natural ability is a prerequisite to human responsibility and that apart from natural ability humans could not be blamed for their failure to obey God.[77] But is Edwards's concept of natural ability actually consistent with genuine ability? If it is not, then this would seem to create problems for his view of human responsibility.

By natural ability, Edwards meant that humans are not subject to any "impeding defect or obstacle that is extrinsic to the will," whether such defect lay in the faculty of understanding, the constitution of body, or in some external object.[78] In Edwards's view, humans possess everything they need to perform the spiritual duties for which they are accountable. The only thing they are lacking is the will to perform such duties.[79]

There are two main difficulties with Edwards's explanation of natural ability. The first problem is that mere possession of some of the faculties to obey God is not the same as the ability to actually do so. Properly speaking, ability is the efficient power to do something.[80] An ability which cannot perform the thing in view is not genuine ability at all and should not be called such.[81] As A. A. Hodge noted, "To say that a dead bird has muscular ability to fly, and only lacks vital ability, is trifling with words."[82] Edwards's notion of natural ability more closely resembles potential capacity than actual ability.[83] And therefore his concept of natural ability does not solve the objection raised by Arminians concerning the issue of inability and responsibility. As Shedd pointed out,

> [Edwards'] great object in the controversy was to establish the doctrine of *inability*. When, however, he is pushed by his opponents with the objection, that if there be no power in fallen man to keep the divine law there is no obligation to keep it, instead of recurring, as the elder Calvinists did, to the fall in Adam and the loss of ability by free act of will, Edwards meets the objection by asserting that fallen man is under no "natural *inability*" to keep

---

77. Edwards, *Freedom of the Will*, 309–10.
78. Edwards, *Freedom of the Will*, 159.
79. Edwards, *Freedom of the Will*, 162.
80. Shedd, *Dogmatic Theology*, 2:225.
81. Hodge, *Systematic Theology*, 2:265. Gerstner argued that Edwards's concept of moral inability is actually a natural inability due to Edwards's understanding of the fall (John H. Gerstner, *The Rational Biblical Theology of Jonathan Edwards*, 3 vols. [Powhatan, VA: Berea, 1991–93] 2:357).
82. Hodge, *Outlines of Theology*, 341.
83. Shedd, *Dogmatic Theology*, 2:225–26.

the divine law, and in this way implies that he has a "natural *ability*" to keep it. But when his definition of the "natural ability" thus *indirectly* attributed to fallen man is examined, it proves not to be efficient and real power, but only a quasi-ability that is incapable of producing the effect required in the objection, namely, perfect obedience. In this way, he evades the objection of his opponent, rather than answers it.[84]

Edwards's failure to address the real issue was noted by the Arminians almost immediately.[85] Edwards had already granted the Arminian premise that responsibility does not exist apart from ability, but the natural ability which Edwards attributed to all humans was not genuine ability and therefore his argument did not actually answer the Arminian objection.[86]

Another difficulty for Edwards's view of natural ability is that it depends upon viewing the natural faculties of humankind apart from their fallen condition. The problem with this is that Scripture nowhere describes any part of the fallen human as morally neutral or untouched by sin. Instead, Scripture consistently depicts both the will and the mind of fallen man as depraved. Shedd noted,

Edwards defines "natural inability" as the want of the requisite mental faculties. Consequently "natural *ability*," for him, is the possession of the requisite mental faculties viewed *apart* from their moral state and condition. In so viewing them, he differs from the elder Calvinists, who regarded a mental faculty and its moral condition as inseparable.[87]

As Shedd correctly pointed out, Edwards's decision to describe part of the human constitution in isolation from its moral condition was a small, but very important step away from his Calvinist heritage.[88] This was a move that cracked open the door for the later New Divinity men to begin

---

84. Shedd, *Dogmatic Theology*, 2:222.

85. E.g., Jonathan Mayhew, *Sermons . . . On Hearing the Word* (Boston: Richard Draper, 1755) 302.

86. In fact, because Edwards accepted the Arminian premise that responsibility is based on ability, one could attempt to argue on Edwards's terms that non-elect humans are not culpable for their failure to please God because they lack the genuine ability to do so. Similarly, on his terms one could try to argue that those who do not hear the gospel are not responsible because they lack the natural ability to receive what they have never heard. These deviations from orthodoxy were surely not part of Edwards's intent (and he would have firmly rejected them), but they seem to be logical conclusions which could be derived from his concession that responsibility does not exist apart from natural ability.

87. Shedd, *Dogmatic Theology*, 2:220.

88. *Westminster Confession of Faith*, 6.2, 4.

emphasizing humanity's natural ability rather than humankind's total inability while claiming Edwardsean precedent.[89]

Conclusion

Although Edwards's distinction between natural and moral inability has been accepted by some theologians, his view contains several weaknesses which call into question its usefulness as a theological concept. Edwards employed this distinction throughout his *Freedom of the Will* in an attempt to explain how humanity can be responsible to obey God and yet be unable to do so apart from divine grace. Departing from earlier Calvinists, Edwards conceded to the Arminians that responsibility does not exist apart from ability. But then in explaining his distinction, he described a moral inability which he said was not properly called inability, and he posited a natural ability which was something less than genuine ability. In his own day several Arminians recognized Edwards's concession as undermining his Calvinistic theology. And in the years since, a number of Calvinist theologians have noted the same.

Contrary to Edwards's assertion in *Freedom of the Will*, humanity is not simply like a prisoner that has been released from his bonds but does not want to humble himself before his prince. Rather unregenerate humans are both unwilling *and* completely unable to leave their prison cell because they are dead in sin. They not only refuse to please God. They are depraved in all their faculties and therefore completely unable to do so.

---

89. E.g., Nathanael Emmons, *The Duty of Sinners to Make Themselves a New Heart* (1812), in *The New England Theology: From Jonathan Edwards to Edwards Amasa Park*, ed. Douglas A. Sweeney and Allen C. Guelzo (Grand Rapids: Baker, 2006) 118–22.

4

"He Went About Doing Good"

Eighteenth-Century Particular Baptists on the Necessity of Good Works

MICHAEL A. G. HAYKIN

Introduction

THE MEETING OF THE future Methodist leader Charles Wesley (1707–88) and the Moravian missionary Peter Böhler (1712–75) on February 7, 1738, was a true turning-point in the history of the Church. Böhler was on his way to South Carolina as a missionary and Wesley, who had had some contact with German-speaking Moravians on his one and only trip to America two years earlier and who had also spent time with the Moravian leader Nicholas von Zinzendorf (1700–1760) in the early part of 1737, offered to help Böhler with his English. In his diary, Wesley recorded that it was on Monday, February 20, that he began to teach Böhler English.[1] Very soon, though, Böhler turned their meeting times to other issues, namely, Charles's standing with God. Wesley had been earnest in his commitment to Christian

---

1. It is a privilege to be able to contribute this article to this Festschrift in honor of a dear brother and fellow church historian, Dr. Gerald Priest. The topic of this paper was suggested by a mutual love of the history of the people called Baptists that I share with Dr. Priest.

"The Journal of Charles Wesley, January 5–April 30, 1738," entry for February 20, 1738 (http://wesley.nnu.edu/charles_wesley/journal/1738a.htm).

principles and assiduous in his practice of the Christian faith for nearly a decade, but his view of the Christian life was a moralistic one. Essentially, he viewed salvation as a reward for the doing of good works.

Shortly after meeting Böhler, Wesley fell seriously ill and thought he was dying. Böhler, visiting Wesley, used the opportunity to ask him plainly: "Do you hope to be saved?" When Charles assured him that he did, Böhler enquired further: "For what reason do you hope it?" "Because I have used my best endeavours to serve God," returned Charles. At such an inadequate response Böhler shook his head sadly and said no more. Charles later admitted that he considered Böhler to be most uncharitable and thought to himself, "What are not my endeavours a sufficient ground of hope? Would he rob me of my endeavours? I have nothing else to trust to."[2] Exactly three months after these journal entries of February 24, 1738, however, Wesley began to understand Böhler's perspective that faith alone was foundational for a right standing with God as he himself went through an Evangelical conversion experience.[3]

Although Charles Wesley had now come to view good works as unnecessary for justification, he remained convinced that good works did have a vital role to play in the Christian life. His position is succinctly put in a sermon that he first preached on December 21, 1738, on Titus 3:8:

> We are to insist that a man is justified, that is, forgiven, and accounted righteous by grace only through faith, exclusive of all works and righteousness of his own; then, that he is to evidence this justification by universal obedience; by continually exercising himself unto righteousness. . . . His [i.e., Christ's] righteousness is not imputed to me unless I manifest it by righteousness inherent in me. Whom he justifies, them he also sanctifies. . . . They are good that do good.[4]

What we see here in miniature in the experience and teaching of one of the central figures in the Evangelical Revival is generally characteristic of the Evangelical movement of the eighteenth and nineteenth centuries.

---

2. "The Journal of Charles Wesley," entry for February 24, 1738.

3. On Wesley's conversion, see Gary Best, *Charles Wesley: A Biography* (Peterborough: Epworth, 2006) 84–94.

4. "Sermon 5 Titus 3:8" in Kenneth G. C. Newport, ed., *The Sermons of Charles Wesley* (Oxford: Oxford University Press, 2001) 154–55, 164. Titus 3:8 runs thus: "This is a faithful saying, and these things I will that thou affirm constantly, that they who have believed in God be careful to maintain good works. These things are good, and profitable unto men" (KJV).

Good works, though rejected as necessary for justification, were nevertheless highly prized as evidence of authentic Christianity. Thus, during the eighteenth and nineteenth centuries we find Evangelicals engaged in a myriad of philanthropic enterprises: the establishment of orphanages; organized support for the poor and destitute, widows and immigrants; specific help for the blind and deaf; the education of the illiterate poor; the release of those imprisoned for small debts[5]; the making of barbarous sports like bear-baiting and bull-baiting illegal; and the rectification of the moral dilemmas created by drunkenness and prostitution.[6] David Bebbington quotes an aphorism from Hannah More (1745–1833)—who is rightly portrayed in a recent biography as a founding figure of Victorian values—that neatly sums up this devotion to social action: "Action is the life of virtue, and the world is the theatre of action."[7]

The "Corrupt Antinomian Leaven"

Now, Bebbington could have cited as equally summary a pithy remark by More's contemporary, the Calvinistic Baptist Robert Hall Jr. (1764–1831), who, in an 1802 sermon to his congregation in Cambridge, maintained that "Christian benevolence is the distinguishing badge of the Christian

---

5. As late as the 1820s, for instance, three-quarters of those in Scottish prisons were there because of the harsh debt laws of the time. See Ernest Marshall Howse, *Saints in Politics: The "Clapham Sect" and the Growth of Freedom* (1952 ed.; repr. London: George Allen & Unwin Ltd., 1971) 125.

6. For details, see Kathleen Heasman, *Evangelicals in Action: An Appraisal of Their Social Work in the Victorian Era* (London: Geoffrey Bles, 1962); John Wolffe, ed., *Evangelical Faith and Public Zeal: Evangelicals and Society in Britain 1780–1980* (London: SPCK, 1995); Nigel A. D. Scotland, *Evangelical Anglicans in a Revolutionary Age 1789–1901* (Carlisle, Cumbria/Waynesboro, Georgia: Paternoster, 2004); Ian Randall, *What a Friend We Have in Jesus: The Evangelical Tradition* (Traditions of Christian Spirituality Series; Maryknoll, NY: Orbis, 2005) 155–59; John Wolffe, *The Expansion of Evangelicalism: The Age of Wilberforce, More, Chalmers and Finney* (A History of Evangelicalism 2; Downers Grove, IL: InterVarsity, 2007) 159–227.

Heasman notes that other factors played a role in the emergence of these philanthropic enterprises: the creation of surplus wealth by the industrial revolution, for instance, and the desire by some middle-class women to have employment outside of the home (*Evangelicals in Action*, 286).

7. *Evangelicalism in Modern Britain: A History from the 1730s to the 1980s* (1989 ed.; repr. Grand Rapids: Baker, 1992) 12. See also Randall, *What a Friend We Have in Jesus*, 155–56. The biography is that of Anne Stott, *Hannah More: The First Victorian* (Oxford: Oxford University Press, 2003).

profession."[8] Hall's aphorism is particularly striking in view of the fact that practical Antinomianism was perceived to be a significant problem among his co-religionists, the English Particular Baptists.[9] At the annual meeting of the Baptist churches of the Western Association in 1789, for example, Caleb Evans (1737–91), the Principal of Bristol Baptist Academy, warned the churches of that association about the "poisonous influence of a corrupt Antinomian leaven."[10] Associations of churches in geographical proximity had been a regular feature of Calvinistic Baptist life since the denomination's seventeenth-century beginnings. By the last half of the eighteenth century these associations were holding annual meetings at which representatives of the churches in these associations, usually the pastors and deacons, were meeting for a couple of days along with a good number of the members of the churches. These annual meetings would be marked by times of corporate prayer, fellowship, and occasions for the public preaching of the Scriptures. At some point in the two-day meeting one of the pastors would be chosen to write a letter to all of the churches in the association on behalf of the association itself. It would be ratified, printed after the annual meeting, and sent out as a circular letter. The Western Association, which had existed since 1653, asked Evans to draw up this letter in 1789.[11]

Evans noted that while there were few among their churches who openly denied "the necessity of personal holiness and good works," there were some who critiqued any who were concerned about these as legalists. "If God sees fit to make us holy," he quoted these critics as saying, "he will, and if not, we cannot make ourselves holy." Evans was certain that where such an attitude as this reigned, it would undermine "the necessity of personal holiness and good works." Evans thus plainly warned his readers,

---

8. "Christian Benevolence" in *The Works of the Rev. Robert Hall, A.M.*, eds. Olinthus Gregory and Joseph Belcher (New York: Harper & Brothers, 1854) 4:528.

9. For details, see Robert W. Oliver, *History of the English Calvinistic Baptists 1771–1892: From John Gill to C. H. Spurgeon* (Edinburgh/Carlisle, Pennsylvania: The Banner of Truth Trust, 2006) 112–45.

10. *Circular Letter of the Western Association* (n.p., 1789) 6. On Evans, see Norman S. Moon, "Caleb Evans, Founder of The Bristol Education Society," *The Baptist Quarterly*, 24 (1971–72) 175–90; and Kirk Wellum, "Caleb Evans (1737–1791)" in Michael A. G. Haykin, ed., *The British Particular Baptists 1638–1910* (Springfield, MO: Particular Baptist Press, 1998) 1:212–33.

11. For the early history of this association, see Geoffrey F. Nuttall, "The Baptist Western Association 1653–1658," *The Journal of Ecclesiastical History*, 15 (1964) 213–18. For a less than adequate history of the association up to the mid-nineteenth century, see J. G. Fuller, *A Brief History of the Western Association* (Bristol, 1843).

If you are not made holy by the gospel now, a lover of holiness in your heart and a practiser of it in your life, you may depend upon it you will not be saved by it hereafter. This is a point as clearly revealed as any one in the whole bible. "If any man be in Christ he is a new creature" [2 Cor 5:17]. Without holiness "no man shall see the Lord" [Heb 12:14]. "He that saith I know him and keepeth not his commandments is a liar and the truth is not in him" [1 John 2:4].[12]

The following year the Western Association asked Philip Gibbs (d.1801), the pastor of the Baptist cause in Plymouth, to draw up the annual circular letter. He too warned the churches in the association to be on their guard against "the baneful and pernicious poison of Antinomianism," which he asserted was an error that was all too prevalent in their day and was, in fact, a "growing evil."[13] Gibbs was careful to emphasize that he was not at all referring to the biblical doctrine of justification by faith alone, which had been wrongly attacked in the eighteenth century by opponents of the Evangelical Revival as Antinomianism. Rather, he was speaking of

that horrid doctrine which makes God the author of sin, by charging it on his absolute decrees; and the minister of sin, by denying the sanctification of the Spirit, and substituting the holiness of Christ as imputed for our sanctification; and which further asserts, that God does not punish or chasten his people for sin, though he expressly declares the contrary in his holy word.[14]

As with Caleb Evans's circular letter the previous year, there is a concern here with the denial of the need for a vigorous pursuit of holiness.

---

12. *Circular Letter of the Western Association* (1789) 7. Evans also identified the errors of eternal justification and the "setting aside the law as a rule of life" as also being part of what he termed the "Antinomian heresy" [*Circular Letter of the Western Association* (1789) 8–11, quote from page 9].

13. *On Truth and Error* in John Rippon, ed., *The Baptist Annual Register* (London, 1793) 1:56–57. Gibbs had been converted under the preaching of George Whitefield (1714–70) in 1745. He initially associated himself with the Calvinistic Methodists, but soon became convinced of Baptist principles. In 1748 he began his ministry at the Baptist cause in Plymouth, which prospered under his pastoral care. It is noteworthy that Gibbs had warned of the danger of Antinomianism in the Western Association's circular letter of 1776: see *Circular Letter of the Western Association* (n.p., 1776) 4–5.

For these details, see "Recent Deaths," *The Evangelical Magazine* 9 (1801) 35; W. T. Adey, *The History of the Baptist Church, Kingsbridge, Devon* (n.p., 1899) 11–13; Edwin Welch, *Two Calvinistic Methodist Chapels 1743–1811* (London: London Record Society, 1975) 34–38.

14. *On Truth and Error* in Rippon, ed., *Baptist Annual Register*, 1:56–57.

Gibbs concluded his discussion of this error with an admonition to his readers to "contend earnestly" for the biblical assertion that union with Christ is evidenced "through sanctification and 'holiness, without which no man shall see the Lord' [Heb 12:14]; for 'if any man have not the Spirit of Christ, he is none of his' [Rom 8:9]."[15] By citing the verse from Rom 8 immediately after that from Heb 12, which Evans had also cited in his circular letter, Gibbs is clearly affirming that a sure mark of the indwelling of the Spirit is the pursuit of a holy life and the doing of good works.

"Our Duty to Grow in Grace"

Gibbs's fellow Baptist, John Ryland Jr. (1753–1825), who became a leading figure in the Western Association in the three decades following Gibbs's letter and was a close friend of William Carey (1761–1834), was also deeply exercised by the growth of Antinomianism. In his funeral sermon for Ryland in 1825, Robert Hall noted that there had been "two extremes" against which Ryland had regularly warned believers. One was "Pelagian pride" and the other was "Antinomian licentiousness, the first of which he detested as an insult on the grace of the gospel; the last, on the majesty and authority of the law."[16] The concern with Antinomianism was partly the result of the fact that Ryland, who became the Pastor of Broadmead Baptist Church in Bristol as well as the Principal of Bristol Baptist Academy in 1793—the latter being held by whomever was serving as the Pastor of Broadmead—had been bitterly attacked in the early 1790s by William Huntington (1745–1813) as one who was subverting the gospel of free grace.

A London preacher popular with any who enjoyed a curious and heady mix of bombast, Tory politics, and rancorous denunciation of any who dared to criticize him,[17] Huntington played a significant role in the

---

15. *On Truth and Error* in Rippon, ed., *Baptist Annual Register*, 1:57.

16. "A Sermon, occasioned by the Death of the Rev. John Ryland, D.D." [*The Works of the Rev. Robert Hall, A.M.*, ed. Olinthus Gregory and Joseph Belcher (New York: Harper & Brothers, 1854) 1:221]. For an overview of Ryland's life, see Michael A. G. Haykin, "John Ryland, Jr.—'O Lord, I would delight in Thee': The life and ministry of John Ryland, Jr. appreciated on the 250th anniversary of his birth," *Reformation Today*, 196 (Nov–Dec 2003) 13–20. For Ryland's pneumatology in general, see also Michael A. G. Haykin, "'The Sum of All Good': John Ryland, Jr. and the Doctrine of the Holy Spirit," *Churchman*, 103 (1989) 332–53, from which some of the following discussion has been drawn.

17. For contrasting perspectives on Huntington, see George M. Ella, *William Huntington: Pastor of Providence* (Darlington, Co. Durham: Evangelical Press, 1994) and

propagation of Antinomian principles in the late eighteenth century. Though he was not a Baptist, numerous Baptists imbibed his argument that the moral law should not be considered as a pattern for the Christian life and that any, like Ryland, who did regard it as such were simply nothing more than "Pharisees" and guilty of "undervaluing Christ's imputed righteousness."[18] Huntington was also insistent that the Bible knows only of imputed sanctification and that there is no scriptural basis at all for the doctrine of progressive sanctification. In his words:

> As to sanctification being a progressive work, it is best to consent to the wholesome words of our Lord Jesus Christ, lest we set poor weak believers to inquiring how long this progressive work is to be on the wheels, what part of it is wrought, what measure of it is required, and how much remains to be done: and like Sarah with her bondwoman, they begin to forward the business by the works of the flesh, instead of lying passive to be worked on. "He that believeth shall not make haste" [Isa 28:16], but he that hasteth with his feet sinneth.[19]

There is no evidence that Huntington himself was guilty of practical Antinomianism, but it is quite understandable that opponents like Ryland viewed Huntington's teaching as the foundation of such. As Ryland summed up Huntingtonianism: "[It is] a false gospel, which . . . [promotes] a redemption, not from sin, but from duty. A perseverance, not in grace, but in security. A mere witness of the Spirit, without the works of the Spirit."[20]

Robert W. Oliver, *History of the English Calvinistic Baptists 1771–1892: From John Gill to C. H. Spurgeon* (Edinburgh/Carlisle, PA: The Banner of Truth Trust, 2006) 119–45.

Huntington went so far as to imply that any who strenuously opposed him would be struck dead by God. See John Ryland, *Serious Remarks on the Different Representations of Evangelical Doctrine by the Professed Friends of the Gospel* (Bristol, 1817) 2:39–41. I am thankful to my colleague, Thomas J. Nettles, for making me a photocopy of this important treatise by Ryland.

18. Robert W. Oliver, "The Emergence of a Strict and Particular Baptist Community among the English Calvinistic Baptists, 1770–1850" (Unpublished PhD thesis, London Bible College, 1986) 130; John Ryland, *The Practical Influence of Evangelical Religion* (London, 1819) 38.

Oliver's thesis is essentially the same as his book, *History of the English Calvinistic Baptists*, though not all of the material in the thesis appears in the book and vice versa.

19. Cited Oliver, *History of the English Calvinistic Baptists*, 127. This text appears in a letter directed against Caleb Evans.

20. "The Enmity of the Carnal Mind" [*Pastoral Memorials: Selected from the Manuscripts of the Late Revd. John Ryland, D.D.* (London: B. J. Holdsworth, 1828) 2:12–13]. See also *The Necessity of the Trumpet's Giving a Certain Sound* (Bristol, 1813) 33; "The

It was against the backdrop of this controversy with Antinomianism that Ryland developed a central pneumatological theme in his theology, namely, that the Spirit's work in sanctifying the believer and leading him or her to be the doer of good works is as important as his role in bringing that person to faith in Christ.[21] When "the Spirit has led the soul to Christ," Ryland maintained, "he will also cause him to run in the way of God's commandments."[22] The Spirit enables saved sinners "to conform to the law as a rule of conduct,"[23] to love holiness,[24] to mortify the flesh and its deeds,[25] to exercise "an irreconcilable hatred of all sin, and an insatiable thirst after perfect conformity to the Saviour."[26] Ryland further argued on the basis of 2 Cor 3:18 that Scripture regards this work of sanctification as a progressive work.

> They [Huntington and his followers] deny that sanctification is progressive, or that it is our duty to grow in grace. . . . [But] what is intended by our "beholding as in a mirror the glory of the Lord, and being changed into the same image from glory to glory, as by the Spirit of the Lord" (2 Cor 3:18)?[27]

On Not Grieving the Holy Spirit

Running parallel with Ryland's intense concern with holy living and the doing of good works was an equally intense fear of bringing grief to the One

---

Believer's Conflict Distinguished from the Struggle of Natural Conscience" (*Pastoral Memorials*, 2:121): "I am greatly afraid that some modern professors wish to substitute an immediate witness of the Spirit for the extensive and important work of the Spirit. They seem to deny all internal sanctification"; *Serious Remarks*, 2:53, where Ryland notes that "some, of late, deny all internal sanctification. They are for imputed sanctification."

21. For more details of this controversy, see Oliver, *History of the English Calvinistic Baptists*, 112–45.

22. "Remarks on the Quarterly Review, for April 1824, Relative to the Memoirs of Scott and Newton" (*Pastoral Memorials*, 2:349).

23. "The Enmity of the Carnal Mind" (*Pastoral Memorials*, II, 14). See also "The Indwelling of the Spirit" (*Pastoral Memorials*, 2:19).

24. "The Love of the Spirit" (*Pastoral Memorials*, 2:46): "Can a man have the Holy Spirit, and not love holiness? Surely not."

25. *Practical Influence of Evangelical Religion*, 14–17, 28; "The Indwelling of the Spirit" (*Pastoral Memorials*, 2:16–17).

26. "The Indwelling of the Spirit" (*Pastoral Memorials*, 2:19).

27. *Serious Remarks*, 2:54.

who sanctified him and enabled him to do good. In what really amounts to a personal confession, Ryland affirmed: "I earnestly seek the supply of the Spirit [see Phil 1:19], and dread, above all things, grieving him by whom I am 'sealed to the day of redemption' [Eph 4:30]."[28] Allusions to this Pauline admonition from Eph 4 are frequent in Ryland's writings.[29] In fact, preserved among his published sermons there are the notes of an address on this very text entitled "On Grieving the Holy Spirit."[30]

The sermon began by emphasizing that Eph 4:30 implies both the personality and deity of the Spirit. With regard to the latter Ryland stated:

> The greatness of the work here attributed to the Holy Spirit, strongly indicates his divinity: who, but a Divine Person, can conquer human obstinacy, renew the heart, bow the will, regenerate the soul, sanctify it, and seal it to the day of redemption. Surely, then, he is not a mere creature, or super-angelic spirit.[31]

Ryland employs a form of argumentation that had been commonly used since the patristic era. If the Spirit does what only God can do, then he must be God.

Ryland now turned his attention to the clause "sealed unto the day of redemption." The seal of the Spirit, Ryland suggested:

> consists in the impression of the divine image on the soul; really conforming us to God, in the temper of our minds. Without this, no immediate witness would be valid; and with it, it is unnecessary.... This is truly a supernatural and divine work. It requires, indeed, the finger of God, to engrave his image on the soul, where it was totally effaced; to renew the resemblance of his moral perfections, and transform us into the likeness of his dear Son.[32]

---

28. "On Devotedness to Christ" (*Pastoral Memorials*, 2:29).

29. See, for instance, "The Days of Heaven upon Earth" [*Pastoral Memorials: Selected from the Manuscripts of the Late Revd. John Ryland, D.D.* (London: B. J. Holdsworth, 1826) 1:18–19]; "The Love of the Spirit" (*Pastoral Memorials*, 2:44, 46); "Separation from the World" (*Pastoral Memorials*, 2:98); "Obedience the Test of Love of God" (*Pastoral Memorials*, 2:295); "On Steadfastness in Religion" (*Pastoral Memorials*, 2:299); "On Lukewarmness in Religion" (*Pastoral Memorials*, 2:302). Cf. "On Sober-Mindedness" (*Pastoral Memorials*, 2:230): "Dread the thought of not being... led by the Holy Spirit."

30. *Pastoral Memorials*, 2:156–60.

31. *Pastoral Memorials*, 2:157.

32. *Pastoral Memorials*, 2:157–58.

Ryland here understands the seal of the Spirit to be the Spirit's progressive sanctification of the believer and reproduction of the character of Christ in the believer's life. Where this holy life is present, no other witness is needed to attest the reality of salvation. "This seal," Ryland concluded, "is the best proof of our relation to God."[33] Ryland's understanding of the seal of the Spirit has obviously been shaped by his controversy with Antinomianism. Yet, he was right to be skeptical of those who claimed that the Spirit had revealed to them that they were children of God and yet whose lives bore few or no marks of holiness.

The second half of Ryland's sermon on Eph 4:30 is focused on "the danger and evil of grieving the Holy Spirit." Here Ryland worked through a number of items that especially grieve the Spirit. Among those that received mention were duplicity and deceit, all types of moral impurity, neglect of prayer and the Word of God, bitterness, "slighting or undervaluing the Lord Jesus Christ, and his atoning blood and righteousness," and "merely formal attendance on divine ordinances, placing a low value on his work and power, and abusing the doctrine of his influence."[34]

The Influence of Jonathan Edwards

Ryland's very evident concern to please the Spirit in all things is essentially bound up with his view of the vital importance of the Holy Spirit for the believer's life. In a sermon on Luke 11:13[35] Ryland makes the following comment on the difference between this verse and its Matthean parallel, Matt 7:11, which has "good things" instead of "the Holy Spirit":

> Nothing is so excellent, needful, or advantageous [as the Holy Spirit]. In this similar part of our Lord's sermon on the Mount, he had said "good things," indefinitely. Matt. vii.11. Here he tells us what is good, the chief good. . . . The Holy Spirit is equivalent to all good things. No other blessing can be safely enjoyed without him. . . . [T]he Holy Spirit is the chief blessing for which we need to pray. His grace is the sum of all spiritual blessing, which we need infinitely more than any other blessing whatever.[36]

---

33. *Pastoral Memorials*, 2:158.

34. *Pastoral Memorials*, 2:159–60.

35. "If ye then, being evil, know how to give good gifts unto your children, how much more shall your heavenly Father give the Holy Spirit to them that ask him" (KJV)!

36. *Pastoral Memorials*, 1:268, 269.

The theologian who was most influential in the theological and spiritual mentoring of Ryland was undoubtedly the American divine Jonathan Edwards (1703–58). Ryland told fellow Baptist Joseph Kinghorn (1766–1832) in 1790, for instance, that Edwards's writings had been more useful to him than any other human compositions and if he was reduced to keeping but three books out of his entire library, then Edwards's life of David Brainerd, his *A Treatise Concerning Religious Affections*, and *True Religion Delineated* by Edwards's disciple Joseph Bellamy (1719–90) would be the three.[37] Now, there is little doubt that the above text by Ryland is essentially Edwardsean. In Edwards's *An Humble Attempt to Promote Explicit Agreement and Visible Union of God's People in Extraordinary Prayer, for the Revival of Religion and the Advancement of Christ's Kingdom on Earth* (1748), written to promote corporate prayer for revival and which Ryland had read in 1784, Edwards had argued in words very similar to those of Ryland:

> The sum of the blessings Christ sought by what He did and suffered in the work of redemption, was the Holy Spirit. . . . [T]he Holy Spirit, in His indwelling, his influences and fruits, is the sum of all grace, holiness, comfort and joy, or in one word, of all the Spiritual good Christ purchased for men in this world: and is also the sum of all perfection, glory and joy, that He purchased for them in another world.[38]

Thus, to return to Ryland's defense of good works, while Ryland's argument for the vital necessity of good works in the believer's life is ultimately based on the text of Holy Scripture, the influence of Edwards should not be discounted. For example, in *A Treatise Concerning Religious Affections*—a text that Ryland treasured, as noted above—Edwards had delineated twelve signs of authentic Christianity, the last of which was that true spirituality bears visible fruit in the doing of good works.[39] Edwards noted on the basis

---

37. Letter to Joseph Kinghorn, October 1790 [cited Martin Hood Wilkin, *Joseph Kinghorn, of Norwich: A Memoir* (Norwich: Fletcher and Alexander, 1855) 183].

His admiration of Edwards went so far as to name one of his sons "Jonathan Edwards Ryland"! In this, though, he was simply following his own father's lead who had named Ryland's brother after his favorite theologian, Herman Witsius (1636–1708), hence Herman Witsius Ryland.

38. Jonathan Edwards, *Apocalyptic Writings*, ed. Stephen J. Stein (*The Works of Jonathan Edwards*, vol. 5; New Haven: Yale University Press, 1977) 320.

39. For Edwards's discussion of this point, see his *Religious Affections*, ed. John E. Smith (*The Works of Jonathan Edwards*, vol. 2; New Haven: Yale University Press, 1959) 383–461. See also Michael A. G. Haykin, *Jonathan Edwards: The Holy Spirit in Revival* (Darlington, Co. Durham: Evangelical Press, 2005) 134–35.

of Titus 2:14 that Christ's people "not only do good works, but are zealous of good works."[40] Such people make Christianity their main business not only on the Lord's Day, but that which occupies their lives as long as they live.[41] While conscious of the fact that good works cannot save them, they also realize that they cannot be saved without them. Thus, "obedience, good works, good fruits, are to be taken," Edwards concluded, "as a sure evidence to our own consciences of a true principle of grace."[42] So Ryland, preaching in June of 1819 on the same text from Titus 2 from which Edwards had derived this emphasis on good works, can state in good Edwardsean fashion:

> As the hand cannot move if there be no motion in the heart, as the superstructure cannot stand without the foundation; so there can be no true holiness without faith in Christ. But of what use is the beating of the heart, if it doth not impel the blood through the whole body? or of what use is the firmest foundation, if no superstructure is to be raised upon it? "He that saith he abideth in" Christ, "ought himself also so to walk, even as he walked" [1 John 2:6]. "For as many as are led by the Spirit of God, they are the sons of God" [Rom 8:14]. And every one in whom a good work is begun, will be solicitous to have it carried on. He will not be satisfied with continued safety, but will long for progressive sanctification.[43]

Salvation by grace alone and a life of good works, "evangelical religion and holy practice," are thus "inseparably connected."[44]

Abolishing Slavery—A Good Work

Ryland's desire to see lives marked by good works among his fellow Baptists did not go unrequited. As was noted at the beginning of this paper, there were a significant array of ways in the late eighteenth and nineteenth centuries in which Baptists as part of the Evangelical movement sought to do good. The outstanding illustration in Ryland's day of such, though, has to be the role that English Baptists played first in the titanic struggle to bring

---

40. Edwards, *Religious Affections*, 387.
41. Edwards, *Religious Affections*, 383–84.
42. *Religious Affections*, 424.
43. *Practical Influence of Evangelical Religion*, 28.
44. *Practical Influence of Evangelical Religion*, 29, 28.

about the abolition of the slave trade and then in the emancipation of the slaves within the British Empire.[45]

Consider the 1824 tract by Robert Hall Jr., *An Address on the State of Slavery on the West India Islands*.[46] Hall had addressed the issue of the slave-trade in the late 1780s when he was first at Bristol serving as co-pastor with Caleb Evans at Broadmead. On that occasion, Hall had two newspaper articles published in the *Bristol Gazette*,[47] in which he maintained that slave-trading is utterly "inhuman," a "trafficking in blood" that is building an "empire of barbarity and ignorance." Hall was well aware of those who would defend the economic necessity of slavery, but he was convinced that "it is almost an insult on the use of language and the art of reasoning to attempt its vindication."[48] It would be close to twenty years later, on February 23, 1807, that the abolitionist forces triumphed and the British parliament overwhelmingly voted to abolish the slave trade, 283 votes to 16. Slavery, though, continued to exist within the bounds of the British Empire. More than a quarter of a century would pass before it too was abolished by parliamentary fiat in the summer of 1833. In the latter campaign to abolish slavery itself, Robert Hall was asked by the Leicester Auxiliary Anti-Slavery Society—Hall was pastoring in Leicester at the time—to compose a tract against slavery, which was published anonymously in 1824.

Hall argued that if the slave trade was deemed to be fundamentally wrong, so was the keeping of slaves. Like the slave trade, it was "most iniquitous in its origin, most mischievous in its effects, and diametrically opposed

---

45. See, for example, the discussion of the former in Michael A. G. Haykin, *Abraham Booth and his Sermon against the Slave Trade* (Dunstable, Bedfordshire: The Strict Baptist Historical Society, 2006).
For the latter, see especially the discussion of the life and ministry of William Knibb (1803–45) in John Howard Hinton, *Memoir of William Knibb, Missionary in Jamaica* (London: Houlston and Stoneman, 1847); Philip Wright, *Knibb "the Notorious": Slaves' Missionary 1803–1845* (London: Sidgwick & Jackson, 1973); Gordon A. Catherall, "William Knibb and Jamaica: The Man Who Spoke Too Strongly" in R. L. Greenall, ed., *The Kettering Connection—Northamptonshire Baptists and Overseas Missions* (Leicester: Department of Adult Education, University of Leicester, 1993) 55–67.

46. *Works of the Rev. Robert Hall*, 2:159–68. On Robert Hall Jr., see Olinthus Gregory, "A Brief Memoir of the Rev. Robert Hall, A.M." in *Works of the Rev. Robert Hall*, 3:3–75; and G. W. Hughes, *Robert Hall (1764–1831)* (London: Independent Press, 1961).

47. For these articles with commentary, see Timothy Whelan, "Robert Hall and the Bristol Slave-Trade Debate of 1787–1788," *The Baptist Quarterly* 38 (1999–2000) 212–24.

48. Whelan, "Robert Hall and the Bristol Slave-Trade Debate," 218–20, *passim*.

to the genius of Christianity."⁴⁹ The West Indian slave owners, though, had convinced themselves that such a system—which treated fellow human beings as "mere beasts of burden, divested of the essential characteristics of humanity," essentially a trampling on "the image of their Maker"—was not unjust. But such reasoning, from Hall's perspective, revealed only a "vitiated" sense of right and wrong.⁵⁰ Slavery and Britain's enjoyment of its fruit—West India sugar, that "ingredient which sweetens our repasts"—was nothing less than worshipping at the "altar of Moloch," a biting reference to the Canaanite idol who demanded human sacrifice.⁵¹

For Hall, to remain silent in the face of "the most enormous oppression exercised within the limits of the British dominions" was to incur guilt along with the slave-owners. As he argued, "we are always answerable for the evils which it is in our power to prevent."⁵² Anticipating that some might reply that only political power could effect the destruction of slavery and the emancipation of the slaves, Hall recalled for his readers the way in which popular support played a determinative role in the abolition of the slave trade.

> We cannot remain silent and inactive, without forgetting who we are, and what we have done; that we are the country which, after a tedious struggle with a host of prejudices arrayed in support of opulent oppression, have overthrown the slave-trade, torn it up by the roots, and branded in the eyes of all nations the sale of human flesh, as the most atrocious of social crimes. . . . We must sever ourselves from all alliance of spirit with a [William] Wilberforce and a [Thomas] Clarkson, who looked forward to the final emancipation of the negro race as the consummation of their labours, and were sustained in their arduous contest by the joy which that prospect inspired. We must lose sight of still more awful considerations, and forget our great Original, who hath formed of "one blood all nations of men, to dwell on all the face of the earth" [Acts 17:26].

Hall's passionate concern to see the abolition of slavery was also rooted in his fear that God would judge his nation severely for their role in maintaining the wicked institution. As he said publicly in the late 1820s, "slavery . . . is

---

49. *Works of the Rev. Robert Hall*, 2:164–65.
50. *Works of the Rev. Robert Hall*, 2:163.
51. *Works of the Rev. Robert Hall*, 2:162, 166.
52. *Works of the Rev. Robert Hall*, 2:168, 167.

the darkest and foulest blot that ever stained the national escutcheon; and, if not speedily wiped out, will call down the vengeance of heaven."[53]

A Concluding Word

Five years after this tract appeared, Hall preached a sermon on November 5, 1829, that dealt with what he called the "Duty of Believers to Maintain Good Works." It was based on Titus 3:8, the very same text that Charles Wesley had preached on some ninety years earlier and with which this paper began. Among the various comments Hall made on this text, he, like Wesley, stressed that Christians must "maintain good works of benevolence to others." They must take care of widows and orphans. They need to help those who are strangers. And those who have wealth must assist those afflicted by poverty. In sum, they are "to excel in deeds of charity" and be imitators of Jesus Christ, whose character is well summed up by the declaration of Acts 10:38, "he went about doing good."[54]

Hall, who, like Ryland, was a lifelong admirer of the writings of Jonathan Edwards,[55] then summed up his remarks in true Edwardsean fashion:

> It is the character of Christian love, that it attends to the infirmities and distresses of others; an eminent Christian will always be eminent in these evidences of genuine charity. It is the effect of spirituality to make the heart tender and generous, feelingly awake to the calls of philanthropy.[56]

---

53. Cited Fred Trestrail, *Reminiscences of College Life in Bristol During the Ministry of the Rev. Robert Hall, A.M.* (London: E. Marlborough and Co., [1879]) 84.

54. "Duty of Believers to Maintain Good Works" in *Works of the Rev. Robert Hall*, 4:253–54.

55. Gregory, "Brief Memoir of the Rev. Robert Hall" in *Works of the Rev. Robert Hall*, 3:65.

56. "Duty of Believers to Maintain Good Works" in *Works of the Rev. Robert Hall*, 4:254.

5

"To Declare the Whole Counsel of God"

Andrew Fuller (1754–1815) on Preaching[1]

Allen R. Mickle, Jr.

Historians of homiletics are divided about the preaching of Andrew Fuller (1754–1815), the Particular Baptist Pastor of Kettering, Northamptonshire, who is probably best known for his critique of hyper-Calvinism in his *The Gospel Worthy of All Acceptation* (1785; 2nd ed., 1801), and for being the founding secretary of the Baptist Missionary Society (BMS) that sent William Carey (1761–1834) to India.[2] The Southern

---

1. This article was originally presented as a paper by Allen Mickle at the Mid-West Regional Meeting of the Evangelical Theological Society in Chicago, IL, March 28–29, 2008. It is with great pleasure and with much appreciation that I dedicate this article to Dr. Gerald Priest. Dr. Priest taught me both homiletics and church history and therefore this topic of Andrew Fuller's theology of preaching is completely appropriate for honoring Dr. Priest. My abilities as a pastor and preacher and as an amateur student of church history have been profoundly influenced by Dr. Priest. May he continue even in his retirement to mold students to become effective ministers of the Gospel and lovers of the faith once for all delivered to the saints.

2. For two excellent theological reflections on Fuller, see the works by Peter J. Morden: *Offering Christ to the World: Andrew Fuller (1754–1815) and the Revival of Eighteenth Century Particular Baptist Life*, Studies in Baptist History and Thought (Milton Keynes, UK: Paternoster, 2003) and *The Life and Thought of Andrew Fuller (1754–1815)*, Studies in Evangelical History and Thought (Milton Keynes, UK: Paternoster, 2015).

The first edition of *The Gospel Worthy of All Acceptation* was published in 1785, and the second with some substantive changes in 1801. For an excellent study of the book and

Baptist historian of homiletics E. C. Dargan (1852–1930), was of the opinion that there was "little warmth—no heat" in Fuller's sermons. Fuller's "imagination is scarcely in evidence at all" in his preaching and "flights of eloquence" are never to be found. Dargan did grant that the sermons are "orderly, discriminating, logical" and his expositions "careful and plain" with a style that was "clear and even." Taken as a whole, though, they lack "grace, fervor, and movement. Excellent good sense and timeliness for their day characterize the writings of Fuller, and they did good and enduring service; but they have not enough literary quality to make them standards."[3] On the other hand, T. Harwood Pattison (1838–1904), well-known for a number of works he wrote on preaching, was convinced:

> His own sermons were weighty, logical, and grave; he had not the finish of [John] Foster nor the splendor of [Robert] Hall, but his simple and vigorous style expressed simple and vigorous thought; that he was an effective preacher may be inferred from the fact that when Thomas Chalmers listened to him he resolved to so far make Fuller model that he would never again read a sermon, but henceforth trust to extemporaneous delivery.[4]

As his own son, Andrew Gunton Fuller, who heard Fuller preach regularly, commented: "Sleepy hearers were not often found in Mr. Fuller's congregation."[5] Fuller may not have been the best of preachers, but, given

---

the controversy surrounding it, see Gerald L. Priest, "Andrew Fuller, Hyper-Calvinism, and the 'Modern Question,'" in *"At the Pure Fountain of Thy Word": Andrew Fuller as an Apologist*, ed. Michael A. G. Haykin, Studies in Baptist History and Thought (Milton Keynes, UK: Paternoster, 2004) 43–73.

For the BMS, see Brian K. Stanley, *The History of the Baptist Missionary Society, 1792–1992* (Edinburgh, UK: T & T Clark, 1992). Literature on Carey is incredibly prolific. Two excellent biographical sources on Carey are Timothy George, *Faithful Witness: The Life and Mission of William Carey* (Birmingham, AL: New Hope, 1991) and S. Pearce Carey, *William Carey*, 3rd ed. (London: The Wakeman Trust, 1993).

3. *A History of Preaching* (New York: George H. Doran, 1912) II, 333.

4. *The History of Christian Preaching* (Philadelphia: American Baptist Publication Society, 1903) 287. In contrast to Dargan, Pattison is right to state that "Andrew Fuller had such a conception of the solemnity of his office as certainly deserves our imitation, whatever we may think of his method of preaching (*History of Christian Preaching*, 287). See also the extended comments on Fuller's preaching from Morris' biography: J. W. Morris, *Memoirs of the Life and Writings of the Rev. Andrew Fuller, late Pastor of the Baptist Church in Kettering, and Secretary to the Baptist Missionary Society* (High Wycombe, 1816) 81–82. Morris notes that he was a popular preacher but that he was not the most eloquent.

5. Andrew Gunton Fuller, *Men Worth Remembering: Andrew Fuller* (London: Hodder

his theological stature, his hard work in preparing messages full of the Scriptures week in and week out, and his earnest pleadings for people to respond in faith to the entirety of the Word of God, his reflections on preaching bear serious reflection. Those reflections are best found in a series of four letters that Fuller wrote in the latter years of his life to a young man in pastoral ministry.[6]

Letter 1: Expounding the Scriptures

Fuller begins his first letter by addressing the great importance of preaching.

> To declare the whole counsel of God in such a way as to save yourself and them that hear you—or, if they are not saved, to be pure from their blood—is no small matter. The character of the preaching in an age contributes, more than most other things, to give a character to the Christians of that age. A great and solemn trust, therefore, is reposed in us, of which we must shortly give an account.[7]

For Fuller, the proclamation of the Word of God was the supreme duty and responsibility of the Christian minister.

Expositional Preaching

Fuller went on to emphasize that preaching should be primarily expositional in nature. While he acknowledged a difference between two types of preaching—"expounding the Scriptures" and "discoursing on Divine subjects," which Fuller appears to understand as topical preaching on particular

---

and Stoughton, 1882) 80.

6. *Thoughts on Preaching*, in *Letters to a Young Minister* in *The Complete Works of the Rev. Andrew Fuller: With a Memoir of His Life*, by Andrew Gunton Fuller, revised by Joseph Belcher (1845 ed.; repr. Harrisonburg, VA: Sprinkle, 1988) 1:712–25. The letters actually have two different recipients, the first three being sent to one minister, and the fourth to another (*Thoughts on Preaching* [*Complete Works of the Rev. Andrew Fuller*, 1:723, note]). In this edition of Fuller's works, the editor adds a fifth piece written by Fuller to *The Evangelical Magazine* entitled "The Abuse of Allegory in Preaching." This short piece is not dealt with in this essay because it focuses more on the interpretation of the Scriptures rather than the proclamation of it (*Thoughts on Preaching* [*Complete Works of the Rev. Andrew Fuller*, 1:726–27]).

7. *Thoughts on Preaching* (*Complete Works of the Rev. Andrew Fuller*, 1:712).

subjects[8]—it was biblical exposition that he found most effective. He writes: "I have found it not a little useful, both to myself and to the people, to appropriate one part of every Lord's Day to the *exposition* of a chapter, or part of a chapter, in the sacred writings."[9] In a letter to his friend John Ryland Jr. (1753–1825), who was principal of the Bristol Baptist Academy,[10] Fuller gave the following advice regarding the students and their preaching:

> I wish they may so believe and feel and preach the truth, as to find their message an important reality, influencing their own souls and those of others. Let them beware of so preaching doctrine as to forget to declare *all* the counsel of God, all the precepts of the Word. Let them equally beware of so dwelling upon the perceptive part of Scripture as to forget the grand principles on which alone it can be carried into effect.[11]

In another place, Fuller noted how effective expositional preaching could be in his own ministry. "In going over a book, I have frequently been struck with surprise in meeting with texts which, as they had always occurred to me, I had understood in a sense utterly foreign from what manifestly appeared to be their meaning when viewed *in connexion with the context*."[12]

Fuller's focus on expositional preaching is the result of his understanding that Scripture alone is to undergird the life of the Church.[13] Fuller could write elsewhere, "Let not the sleight of wicked men, who lie in wait

---

8. *Thoughts on Preaching* (*Complete Works of the Rev. Andrew Fuller*, 1:712).

9. *Thoughts on Preaching* (*Complete Works of the Rev. Andrew Fuller*, 1:712), emphasis in the original.

10. For more on Ryland, see Michael A. G. Haykin, "John Ryland, Jr.—'O Lord, I would delight in Thee': The life and Ministry of John Ryland, Jr. appreciated on the 250th anniversary of his birth," *Reformation Today*, 196 (Nov–Dec 2003) 13–20.

11. Cited in Michael A. G. Haykin, ed., *The Armies of the Lamb: The Spirituality of Andrew Fuller* (Dundas, ON: Joshua, 2001) 161. This letter, dated April 5, 1798, is taken from John Ryland, Jr., *The Work of Faith, the Labour of Love, and the Patience of Hope, Illustrated; In the Life and Death of the Reverend Andrew Fuller* (London: Button & Son, 1816) 379–80.

12. *Thoughts on Preaching* (*Complete Works of the Rev. Andrew Fuller*, 1:712), emphasis in the original.

13. See the helpful section on the priority of Scripture in Fuller's thought in Paul Brewster, "The Theological Method of Andrew Fuller," *Eusebeia: The Bulletin of the Jonathan Edwards Centre for Reformed Spirituality* 6 (Spring 2006) 41–48. For an examination of the way that Fuller viewed the Scriptures, see Michael Haykin, "'The Oracles of God': Andrew Fuller and the Scriptures," *Churchman* 103:1 (1989) 60–76.

to deceive, nor even the pious character of good men (who yet may be under great mistakes), draw me aside. Nor do thou suffer my own fancy to guide me. Lord, thou hast given me a determination to take up no principle at second hand; but to search for everything at the pure fountain of thy word."[14] For Fuller, the Scriptures were the "oracles of God."[15] They were direct revelation from God and nothing was more authoritative in the life of the believer or God's people than the Word of God.[16] It was this high view of the Scriptures that led Fuller, it appears, to emphasize the necessity of proclaiming the Scriptures verse by verse and chapter by chapter.

Fuller contrasts this expositional way of preaching with a form that appears to have been far too prevalent in his Baptist circles, namely, taking a text of Scripture out of context by interpreting it in light of other passages that contain the same words. He writes:

> If the hearer, when you have done, understand no more of that part of Scripture than he did before, your labour is lost. Yet this is commonly the case with those attempts at expounding which consist of little else than comparing parallel passages, or, by the help of a Concordance, tracing the use of the same word in other places, going from text to text till both the preacher and the people are wearied and lost. This is troubling the Scriptures rather than expounding them.[17]

To simply develop a line of argument from a verse by undertaking what amounts to word studies is hardly the way to present the true meaning of a verse. The text must be understood in its literary context. For Fuller, an approach to preaching that was anything less than understanding the text in its context was not truly preaching.

---

14. Ryland, *Life and Death of the Reverend Andrew Fuller*, 203–4.

15. Andrew Fuller, *The Nature and Importance of an Intimate Knowledge of Divine Truth* (*Complete Works of the Rev. Andrew Fuller*, 1:160).

16. "Fuller believed the Bible was revelation from God. Its words are inspired so that they are infallible and free from error. Therefore we should venerate them, study them, and submit all our thought and deeds to their authority. Whenever Fuller opposed the heresies of his day, or when he was advising his fellow believers, his appeal was always to the truth of Scripture" (L. Russ Bush and Tom J. Nettles, *Baptists and the Bible*, rev. ed. [Nashville: Broadman and Holman, 1999] 99–100).

17. *Thoughts on Preaching* (*Complete Works of the Rev. Andrew Fuller*, 1:712).

The State of the Preacher

While the mechanics of preaching were important to Fuller, the spiritual state of the preacher himself was just as vital. Fuller writes, "Moreover, to enter into the true meaning of the Scriptures, it is absolutely necessary that we *drink into the spirit* of the writers. . . . It is impossible to enter into the sentiments of any great writer without a kindred mind."[18] Fuller is quick to clarify that this does not come about by some kind of "extraordinary inspiration" but that it comes through the ordinary work, as it were, of the Holy Spirit. The Spirit works through the life of the minister to change him and conform his mind more and more to that of Christ. A spiritual mind that is focused on Christ, Fuller believes, is one that is capable of best understanding the meaning of the Scriptures.

Not only does the Spirit work in the preacher's mind to better understand the Scriptures that he is studying, but understanding one portion of God's Word opens up doors to understand other areas of the Bible. "It is thus also that a lively faith in the sufferings of Christ, and the glory arising out of them, is a key which unlocks a large part of the sacred oracles. While the disciples remained ignorant of his death, they knew but little of the Scriptures but, having learned the design of this great event, a flood of light poured in upon them, and the Old Testament became plain and deeply interesting."[19]

Moreover, a humble understanding of his ignorance of so much of the Bible causes a preacher to rely more upon God and thus arrive at the meaning of a verse or passage not through his own efforts, but through the illumination of God. As Fuller observes in this regard, "There are few things which tend more to blind the mind than a conceit of our own powers."[20] Fuller himself was an autodidact with regard to theology, and he well understood the way that knowledge, albeit vital for ministry, can become a major hindrance by its stimulation of pride and arrogance.

---

18. *Thoughts on Preaching* (*Complete Works of the Rev. Andrew Fuller*, 1:713).
19. *Thoughts on Preaching* (*Complete Works of the Rev. Andrew Fuller*, 1:713).
20. *Thoughts on Preaching* (*Complete Works of the Rev. Andrew Fuller*, 1:713).

Once for All Delivered to the Saints

The Student of the Scriptures and Others

Fuller highlights the fact that it is necessary not only to study the Scriptures for the sake of proclaiming them but also to have them personally change the student and preacher. He writes,

> To understand the Scriptures in such a manner as profitably to expound them, it is necessary to be conversant with them in private; and to mix, not only faith, but the prayer of faith, with what we read. There is a great difference between reading the Scriptures *as a student*, in order to find something to say to the people, and reading them *as a Christian*, with a view to get good from them for one's own soul.[21]

Here Fuller is warning against the danger of what some in the modern world would call "professionalism." The preacher can so easily become a professional, going through the motions of preaching in a way that is removed from his own personal life, and the result will be hypocrisy. The message of the text must grip the heart of the preacher before he brings it to the pulpit. There must be fire and light in the heart of the preacher before the same can be found in the congregation.

What place do commentaries on the Scriptures have in the preacher's preparation? Though Fuller believes it wrong to go to commentators like the polymath John Gill (1697–1771) of his own Baptist community prior to doing the tough work of exegesis, it is not at all wrong to consult them. Fuller argues that after one has sought to understand the Scriptures one can then turn to able expositors. But, to go first to the secondary sources "is to preclude the exercise of your own judgment; and, after all that which is furnished by the labours of another, though equally good in itself, will be far less interesting to us than that which is the result of our own application."[22]

Finally, in this first letter, Fuller notes that the preacher needs to keep notes of his sermons so he can review them before going into the pulpit and so that he also has them for future use.

---

21. *Thoughts on Preaching* (*Complete Works of the Rev. Andrew Fuller*, 1:713–14), emphasis in original.

22. *Thoughts on Preaching* (*Complete Works of the Rev. Andrew Fuller*, 1:714).

Letter 2: Sermons—Their Subject Matter

In this second letter, Fuller addresses the subject matter of sermons and the manner in which this content is to be addressed to their hearers.

The Matter of Preaching

Fuller first discusses the content of the sermon, an extremely important matter to him. He argues that unless "the subject matter of your preaching be truly evangelical, you had better be anything than a minister."[23] But what exactly does Fuller mean by "evangelical" here? He explains it a little by what follows this quote: it is preaching the gospel. In another context, he described this as setting before one's hearers the fact that they "should believe that Jesus is the Christ, the Son of God, and believing, have life through his name."[24] Every sermon must ultimately lead to Jesus Christ. As Fuller writes elsewhere, "Every sermon, more or less, should have some relation to Christ, and bear on his person or work. . . . However ingenious our sermons may be, unless they bear on Christ, and lead the mind to Christ, we do not preach the faith of the gospel."[25]

For support for this conviction, Fuller argues that the New Testament in various places clearly commands the minister to preach the gospel: "Preach the word.—Preach the gospel.—Preach the gospel to every creature," etc.[26] This leads Fuller to make four concrete conclusions regarding both the manner and matter of preaching.

The Manner of Preaching

First, Fuller reckons that in every sermon, preachers "should have an errand; and one of such importance that if it be received or complied with it will issue in eternal salvation."[27] The preacher has to do more than simply

---

23. *Thoughts on Preaching* (*Complete Works of the Rev. Andrew Fuller*, 1:714).

24. Andrew Fuller, *The Gospel Worthy of All Acceptation* (2nd ed.; Boston: American Doctrinal Tract Society, 1837) 6. Fuller here is quoting John 10:31.

25. *Faith in the Gospel Essential to Preaching It* (*Complete Works of the Rev. Andrew Fuller*, 1:516).

26. *Thoughts on Preaching* (*Complete Works of the Rev. Andrew Fuller*, 1:715).

27. *Thoughts on Preaching* (*Complete Works of the Rev. Andrew Fuller*, 1:715), emphasis in original.

try to reshape the moral values of his hearers; he must think about his task in these terms: "I am expected to preach, it may be to some hundreds of people, some of whom may come several miles to hear; and what have I to say to them? Is it for me to sit here studying a text merely to find some thing to say to fill up the hour? I may do this . . . without winning, or even aiming to win, one soul to Christ."[28] In other words, at the core of his preaching must be a passion for the salvation of the lost. Thus, each sermon must, in some way, should drive home the realization that men and women apart from Jesus Christ are lost.

In the next place, Fuller avers, "every sermon should contain a portion of the doctrine of salvation by the death of Christ."[29] For a sermon to be "a gospel sermon," it must contain at some point reference to the cross-work of Christ. This point and the one before seem to be what is meant by preaching the gospel, which Fuller had emphasized in the previous letter.

Third: "In preaching the gospel, we must not imitate the orator, whose attention is taken up with his performance, but rather the herald, whose object is to publish, or proclaim, good tidings."[30] Fuller himself was a great example in this regard. As noted at the beginning of this essay, Fuller was not a great orator, but there is no doubt that his contemporary hearers found him to be a powerful herald of the gospel in his day. To hear Fuller was to come away with the conviction that this man truly believes what he is preaching.

Finally, "though the doctrine of reconciliation by the blood of Christ forms the ground-work of the gospel embassy, yet it belongs to the work of the ministry, not merely to declare that truth, but to accompany it with earnest calls, and pressing invitations, to sinners to receive it, together with the most solemn warnings and threatenings to unbelievers who shall continue to reject it."[31] The preacher of the gospel must use various means—warnings and divine threatenings, pleadings and urgent appeals—to win the lost.[32] This was a hallmark of Fuller's ministry.

---

28. *Thoughts on Preaching* (*Complete Works of the Rev. Andrew Fuller*, 1:715–16).
29. *Thoughts on Preaching* (*Complete Works of the Rev. Andrew Fuller*, 1:716).
30. *Thoughts on Preaching* (*Complete Works of the Rev. Andrew Fuller*, 1:716).
31. *Thoughts on Preaching* (*Complete Works of the Rev. Andrew Fuller*, 1:717).
32. Fuller, though, is clear that the work of salvation belongs solely to God not to the preacher of the Gospel: "Though we invite men, yet it is not on their pliability that we must rest our hopes, but on the power and promise of God" (*Thoughts on Preaching* [*Complete Works of the Rev. Andrew Fuller*, 1:717).

Letter 3: The Composition of a Sermon (Part 1)

In the next letter, Fuller moves on to address the details of the composition of a sermon. Again, he emphasizes that the spiritual frame of the preacher is critical for the impact of the sermon. "Spirituality of mind," as he terms it, is thus vital in the composition and delivery of sermons: "the first thing . . . before we sit down to study, should be to draw near to God in prayer."[33] Fuller reminds the preacher that he should not aspire to "great elegance of expression."[34] A second initial remark that Fuller makes is that the preacher must take care to communicate his message in a way for all to understand and not just a select few. Fuller writes:

> We ought to use sound speech, and good sense; but if we aspire after great elegance of expression, or become very exact in the formation of our periods, though we may amuse and please the ears of a few, we shall not profit the many, and consequently shall not answer the great end of our ministry. Illiterate hearers may be very poor *judges* of preaching; yet the effect which is produces upon them is the best criterion of its real excellence.[35]

Following these initial caveats, Fuller outlines the various elements of the sermon construction process:

1. Study the text in its Scriptural context to arrive at its original meaning.
2. Once the meaning of the text has been determined, turn to the commentators to provide additional light.
3. But when all this is said and done, "Be satisfied, at all events, that you have the mind of the Holy Spirit before you proceed."[36]
4. Take note of the significant individual words in the text being preached.
5. At this point, the preacher should have a number of leading ideas, but going forward he needs to stress one main idea in his sermon; as he notes: "Many sermons are a *mob* of ideas; they contain very good sentiments, but they have no object in view. . . . What is it you are aiming

---

33. *Thoughts on Preaching* (*Complete Works of the Rev. Andrew Fuller*, 1:717–18).
34. *Thoughts on Preaching* (*Complete Works of the Rev. Andrew Fuller*, 1:717).
35. *Thoughts on Preaching* (*Complete Works of the Rev. Andrew Fuller*, 1:717).
36. *Thoughts on Preaching* (*Complete Works of the Rev. Andrew Fuller*, 1:718).

at? What is this to the purpose?... Unity of design... is indispensable to good preaching."[37]

6. Finally, application needs to be made—what Fuller called "improving the subject."[38]

Fuller also gives an extensive example of topical preaching from Ps 145:16 in this letter and illustrates how the various steps he has outlined regarding the sermon process could be concretely applied to a sermon on this text.

The Composition of a Sermon (Part 2)

The fourth and final of Fuller's letters is written to a different individual and Fuller reiterates some of the points of advice that he had touched on in the other letters. A preacher should not memorize his sermon but only commit key thoughts to memory; he should never bring his manuscript into the pulpit. He needs to avoid using vulgar terms or obscure words. He should also avoid having a multitude of points and sub-points (a way of sermon division common among the Puritans).[39] Fuller then provides an example of how he would develop a sermon on Ps 36:9, but stresses that every text "requires a mode of discussion for itself."[40] In other words, while there are certain general principles to guide the preacher in sermon construction (as the ones he has given in this mini-series of reflections on preaching), nevertheless, each sermon will have some unique features.

Conclusion

Andrew Fuller has not been remembered as a scintillating preacher, as was his older contemporary George Whitefield (1714–70). Yet, he faithfully applied himself to preaching the gospel and the Bible for more than forty years, and in that time, he learned a number of valuable lessons that he passed on in these four letters. Thankfully, the printing of these letters in Fuller's collected works gave them a wider audience than the original two young preachers to whom Fuller sent them.

37. *Thoughts on Preaching* (*Complete Works of the Rev. Andrew Fuller*, 1:719), emphasis in original.
38. *Thoughts on Preaching* (*Complete Works of the Rev. Andrew Fuller*, 1:722).
39. *Thoughts on Preaching* (*Complete Works of the Rev. Andrew Fuller*, 1:724).
40. *Thoughts on Preaching* (*Complete Works of the Rev. Andrew Fuller*, 1:725).

6

"A Young Man's Difficulty with His Bible"

Not My Father's Faith

Jeff Straub

Introduction

THE NINETEENTH CENTURY WAS a time of deep theological unrest. Biblical criticism questioned the nature of biblical revelation and Darwinian evolution questioned the historicity and accuracy of the Bible. Many Christians felt a growing pressure to abandon old Christian paths and seek for ways of reading their Bible that would comport with the new critical and scientific views. This unsettled response was keenly felt among the younger generations of Christians. Baptist William Newton Clarke (1841–1912),[1] for example, summarized well the dilemma he and others experienced.

---

1. I have had both the privilege of sitting under Jerry as a professor during my study at Detroit and of working with him more recently as a colleague in church history. We share many of the same historical interests. I hope he will have many years more to contribute to the conversation and I wish him the best in his retirement!

For biographical information in Clarke, see Claude L. Howe Jr. *The Theology of William Newton Clarke* (New York: Arno, 1980). This work was originally submitted as a doctoral thesis at New Orleans Baptist Theological Seminary in 1959. A more comprehensive treatment of Clarke's theology with the best bibliography of Clarke's writings available, though still incomplete, is Bernard Harvey Cochran, "William Newton Clarke: Exponent of the New Theology" (PhD diss., Duke University, 1961). Briefer biographical sketches include William H. Brackney, *The Baptists* (New York: Greenwood, 1988) 143–44; Bill J. Leonard, ed., *Dictionary of Baptists in America* [*DBA*] (Downers Grove,

> With respect to the Bible, I am one of the men who have lived through the crisis of the Nineteenth Century, and experienced the change which that century has wrought. I began, as a child must begin, with viewing the Bible in the manner of my father's day, but am ending with a view that was never possible until the large work of the Nineteenth Century upon the Bible had been done.[2]

Clarke had been reared in a pastor's home[3] with parents who loved and feared God and held a simple belief in an inerrant Bible, typical of old orthodoxy. "All that the Bible said of God or men was true, all that God or good men did was right, and the stories were sacred."[4] Yet soon Clarke was to discover certain "contradictions" contained in the Bible that apparently could not be answered. He believed that geology and Genesis were irreconcilable. He came to hold that his father's faith, simple and sincere though it was, would not stand careful scrutiny. The old views had to give way to new ones lest the Bible be completely cast aside. Biblical criticism and Darwinian evolution informed the way the Bible would need to be read. Not everything in the Bible was of equal value. Some things had to be set aside as antiquated, contradictory, or even wrong. Textual criticism had demonstrated "uncertainty as to the very words" of the text. As a youth, Clarke "looked upon the Bible as so inspired by God that its writers were not capable of error."[5] As time went on, he came to believe that "if we cannot be perfectly sure of the very words that were first written, we cannot claim that any text in our possession is verbally inspired; and as for the idea that there was a verbally inspired and faultless text . . . the wonder is that any one [sic] ever took it seriously at all."[6]

IL: IVP, 1994), s.v. "Clarke, William Newton," by T. Weber; *Dictionary of Christianity in America* [*DCA*], s.v. "Clarke, William Newton," by T. Weber; and James E. Tull, *Shapers of Baptist Thought* (reprinted, Macon: Mercer University Press, 1984) 153–81.

2. William Newton Clarke, *Sixty Years with the Bible* (New York: Charles Scribner's Sons, 1909) 3.

3. William's father was William Clarke. He became pastor at the Baptist church in Cazenovia, New York, in 1835 and was there until 1864 except for a two year hiatus at Whitesboro, New York (1852–54). The Cazenovia church requested his return, and as the educational opportunities for William Newton were better, he consented. On William, the father, see [Emily Clarke], *William Newton Clarke* (New York: Charles Scribner's Sons, 1913) 6ff. William Sr. was, apparently, a self-taught man who earned much of his living by farming.

4. Clarke, *William Newton Clarke*, 16.

5. Clarke, *William Newton Clarke*, 42.

6. Clarke, *William Newton Clarke*, 47.

Other young men felt these same pressures which eventually divided generations and pitted fathers against their sons. Sometimes the sons simply modified the views of their fathers, retaining a form of Christianity in sympathy with the new views, but much to the consternation of their elders. At other times, the sons abandoned the parental views altogether, placing their parents in untenable positions. In 1891, for example, Augustus Hopkins Strong (1836–1921),[7] president of Rochester Theological Seminary and member of First Baptist Church of Rochester, New York, was placed in the difficult circumstance of having to recommend that his son Charles Augustus Strong (1862–1940)[8] be dismissed from the membership of their church because Charles "has so changed his views with regard to essential doctrines that he is no longer in sympathy with the church."[9] Charles, despite an orthodox upbringing, rejected Christianity. He studied at Harvard University, where he came under the influence of William James and became a close friend of George Santayana. Subsequently he gave up all pretext of following his father's religion and became an avowed skeptic.[10] To his dying breath, his father tried to reclaim Charles to the faith.[11]

---

7. For biographical information on A. H. Strong see Augustus Hopkins Strong, *Autobiography of Augustus Hopkins Strong*, edited by Crerar Douglas (Valley Forge, PA: Judson, 1981). Also Carl F. H. Henry, *Personal Idealism and Strong's Theology* (Wheaton, IL: Van Kampen, 1951); and Grant Wacker, *Augustus H. Strong and the Dilemma of Historical Consciousness* (Macon: Mercer University Press, 1985). Shorter sketches on Strong's life include Gregory Alan Thornberry, "Augustus Hopkins Strong," in *Theologians of the Baptist Tradition*, edited by Timothy George and David S. Dockery (Nashville: Broadman and Holman, 2001) 139–69; Kurt A. Richardson, "Augustus Hopkins Strong," in *Baptist Theologians*, edited by Timothy George and David S. Dockery (Nashville: Broadman, 1990) 289–306; *DBA*, "Strong, Augustus Hopkins," by G. Wacker, 262–63; Brackney, *The Baptists*, 269; Brackney, *Historical Dictionary of Baptists* (*HDB*) 402; Clifton J. Allen et al., eds., *ESB*, (Nashville: Broadman, 1958), s.v. "Strong, Augustus Hopkins," by Penrose St. Amant; *Dictionary of Christianity in America*, s.v. "Strong, Augustus Hopkins," by G. Wacker; *Dictionary of American Biography* [*DAB*] 18:142–43; and *American National Biography*, 21:36–37.

8. For biographical information on Charles, see *The General Catalogue of the University of Rochester, 1850–1911* (Rochester: University of Rochester Press, 1911) 78. Also *DAB*, Supplement 2, 638–40.

9. See Minutes of the Prudential Committee, First Baptist Church of Rochester, New York, November 2, 1891. A. H. Strong was the secretary of the Prudential Committee at the time and made the motion to censure. I hope to tell a bit of this story in a forthcoming article.

10. See C. A. Strong, *A Creed for Skeptics* (London: MacMillan, 1936).

11. For evidence of this, see the collection of letters from A. H. Strong to C. A. Strong housed in the Charles Augustus Strong Papers at the Rockefeller Archives Center, Sleepy

Once for All Delivered to the Saints

William N. Clarke and Charles A. Strong were certainly not alone in their unsettled views. Many young men went off to college or seminary, only to leave those schools radically different than when they went in. In some cases, the transition began before they entered these institutions, while at other times, the changes occurred during their years of study. In both cases, however, the denominational schools themselves often served to hasten the theological transitions of the students. Fathers were in a quandary—how should they educate their children in a milieu of radical change and yet hope to have them remain both orthodox and Christian?[12]

Much of the story of the theological transitions from one generation to the next has been lost to historians, discarded as irrelevant, or purposefully destroyed to prevent investigation.[13] However, one participant in this theological shift left a bit more material for historians to delve into. William Herbert Perry Faunce (1859–1930) was the son of a prominent New

---

Hollow, New York. The younger Strong was married to Bessie, the eldest daughter of John D. Rockefeller Sr. The letters cover the last eleven years of the elder Strong's life. The collection contains approximately 400 letters, from Augustus to Charles, some of which include exhortations to recognize the faith that must lie dormant within the younger son's breast. In the process of time, Augustus interceded on behalf of his son Charles, though without Charles's input, to have the church action overturned, which happened in 1916.

12. "I am coming to feel that you might as well send a boy to hell as to send him to a so called Christian college. I know just what I am talking about. Do you know of a so called Christian college where a boy could be sent without putting him under the influence of skeptical teaching, dancing, drunkenness, gambling and licentiousness? It looks as if our college authorities have joined hands with the very worst elements in society under the name of Breadth to win (?) the youth of our land." O. W. Van Osdel to Dr. Hewitt (Charles Edmund), March 9, 1898, University Presidents Papers, 1889–1925, Box 67, Folder 7, Special Collections Research Center, University of Chicago, Chicago, IL. Emphasis in the original. Van Osdel was pastor of the First Baptist Church of Spokane, Washington, at this time but later would become a leader in the fight for orthodoxy among Northern Baptists. See Kevin T. Bauder, "Biography of O. W. Van Osdel," (ThM thesis, Denver Baptist Theological Seminary, 1983). Van Osdel's son, Edgar Bates Van Osdel, studied science at the graduate level at Chicago after finishing his undergraduate degree at Knox College, Galesburg, IL. He abandoned orthodoxy apparently while in a denominational school.

13. It is interesting, for instance, that very little personal material of William Newton Clarke is extant. He and his wife burned his personal papers in his twilight years, fearing that a would-be biographer would fail to nuance the material correctly. Some of what was burned dated from his student days. See [Emily Clarke], *William Newton Clarke: A Biography* (New York: Charles Scribner's Sons, 1916) 126–27. For this reason, Clarke's part in this story comes solely from his autobiographical reminiscences, *Sixty Years with the Bible*.

England clergyman and would become a key figure in Baptist life in the late nineteenth and early twentieth century, during the tumultuous times when theological liberalism attained hegemony among Northern Baptists. His father, Daniel, representing an older orthodoxy, found himself confronted with many young men passing through the fires of theological turmoil. In response, Daniel W. Faunce[14] penned a number of books aimed at confronting these pressing problems. Among them is a book that is incorporated into the title of this paper.

When Daniel wrote *A Young Man's Difficultly with His Bible*,[15] it was no mere pastoral epistle offered to young inquirers hoping to keep them in the faith. It also proved to be rather proleptic of his own effort to dissuade his son from embracing the "new theology."[16] The elder Faunce, as a pastor, began to encounter young men who were pondering progressive views. He received troubling questions that required solid answers and attempted to help those "unsettled in their views of religion" by addressing some of those questions.[17]

> The author, on assuming the pastoral charge of a church in a thrifty and intelligent inland city of New England, found in the community a large number of young men not exactly skeptical

14. Faunce (1829-1911) was born in Plymouth, MA, and descended from John Faunce, an early Plymouth Plantation member who arrived in the New World in 1622. Daniel graduated from Amherst College in 1850 and studied for several years at Newton Theological Institution in 1853 and 1854. While at Newton, he was ordained by the Baptist Church at Somerville, MA, where he pastored for one year. He subsequently served churches in Worcester (1854-60) and Malden, MA (1860-66); Concord, NH (First Baptist, 1866-75); Lynn, MA (Washington Street Baptist, 1875-81); Washington, DC (East Street Baptist, 1881-89); West Newton, MA (1889-93); and finally at Pawtucket, RI (1894-99). From 1899 until his retirement, he remained active in literary work. Biographical information on Faunce may be found in *General Catalogue of the Newton Theological Institution, 1826-1943*, edited by Richard D. Pierce (Newton Centre, MA: The Newton Theological Institution, 1943) 75; William Cathcart, *The Baptist Encyclopedia* (Philadelphia: Louis H. Everts, 1881; rpt. Paris, AR: The Baptist Standard Bearer, 1988) 390; and *Who's Who in America, 1910-1911*, edited by Albert Nelson Marquis (Chicago: A. N. Marquis, Co., 1910) 624-25.

15. Daniel W. Faunce, *A Young Man's Difficulties with His Bible* (New York: Sheldon, 1876).

16. The phrase "new theology" occurs repeatedly in the latter nineteenth century as a common title for theological liberalism then making significant inroads across the theological landscape. For example, see "Baptist Theological Drift," *The Watchman*, June 11, 1891, 4. See also Newman Smyth, "The New Theology," *National Baptist*, June 30, 1887, 403-4.

17. Faunce, *A Young Man's Difficulties*, 5.

but a good deal unsettled in their views of religion. . . . They had caught the drift of one section of popular thought. They asked for some book which should meet briefly and yet fairly the difficulties which they felt.[18]

Ironically, Daniel's own son William, who was sixteen at the time of the book's publication, though younger when the lectures first were given,[19] may well have been experiencing these same challenges. In just a couple of years, William would be in the midst of a crisis of soul that left him doubting his own faith and the direction his life would take.

By 1880, William graduated from Brown University and followed in his father's footsteps into the Baptist ministry. Also like his father, he enrolled in The Newton Theological Institution of Newton, Centre, MA, to prepare for that ministry. While at Newton, he corresponded with his Daniel, expressing a growing restlessness with the traditional views of his youth, and stating a desire to cast them aside and allow the winds of change to fill his sails and carry him whithersoever those winds would blow. His father, responding to the letters privately and perhaps by continuing a public writing ministry, attempted to persuade his drifting son not to stray too far from his inherited faith. It seems more than coincidental that a major concern of the elder Faunce's later writings focused on subjects related to theological orthodoxy, especially after his son William began moving toward liberalism. For example, in 1892, D. W. published *Letters to a Skeptic* in which he dealt with such subjects as miracles, sin, and the atonement. The stated purpose of the book was "the hope that God will use it for guiding some struggling soul through perplexity into faith."[20] For at least the past ten years, William had been such a man. Several years after *Letters* appeared the elder Faunce prepared another book aimed at the kinds of struggles his son continued to face. This time the subject was the doctrine of inspiration. No biblical doctrine was more challenged in early liberalism than divine inspiration, for it was the foundation of many other views. If one could discount the supernatural character of the Bible, then the super-

---

18. Faunce, *A Young Man's Difficulties*, 5.

19. D. W. Faunce indicated that he prepared the lectures for inquirers while at Concord, New Hampshire, and gave them again to inquirers at Lynn, Massachusetts. He does not state during what year he originated the material but he changed pulpits from Concord to Lynn in 1876, the year preceding publication. Faunce, *A Young Man's Difficulties*, 6.

20. D. W. Faunce, *Letters to a Skeptic* (Philadelphia: American Baptist Publication Society, 1892) 3.

natural elements to which it testified—the miracles, for instance—could likewise be eliminated. So the elder Faunce offered a careful discussion on the nature of the Bible and its origin.[21] Finally, Daniel produced a treatise seemingly aimed at the theological downturn his own son's life had taken. In 1908, almost ten years after William became president of Brown University, his father wrote *The Mature Man's Difficulties with His Bible*.[22] Again, the topics included the kinds of issues then being addressed by liberalism such as the relationship between the Bible and science.[23]

The goal of this article is to explore the intergenerational concerns that arose as a result of the theological drift in college and seminary education. Clergyman fathers saw in their sons cause for concern and, seemingly, were helpless to thwart the influences they were receiving toward the new theology. Doubtless many letters of communication were passed between these generations as the new trends were taught, discussed, and embraced. Many of these conflicts are difficult to trace as correspondence has long since been lost. However, in the historical record, a few choice materials remain that suggest the conflict that must have lain beneath the surface. The brief but important record between the elder and younger Faunces will serve as a lens through which to explore this crisis. This is a story that transcended a particular denomination, but for the purposes of narrowing the conversation, I will examine only the Baptist aspect.

The Winds of Change—The Inroads of the New Theology

Theological liberalism began to make inroads into the American scene in the early 19th century as the influences of German higher critical thought made their way into academic life largely through professors who traveled to Europe for advanced theological training. Many Protestants from historically orthodox denominations made the pilgrimage to prestigious universities to study theology under some of the best German thinkers of the day.

---

21. D. W. Faunce, *Inspiration Considered as a Trend* (Philadelphia: American Baptist Publication Society, 1896).

22. Philadelphia: American Baptist Publication Society, 1908.

23. While compelling historical evidence is lacking to argue conclusively that Daniel's subsequent works were written directly because of his own son's wayward beliefs, it seems more than coincidental, when one tracks the younger man's theological pilgrimage, that the older man was arguing in print for the maintenance of the old orthodoxy at the same time the son was abandoning it.

Upon returning to the United States, they incorporated the new views into their classrooms, initiating a process that saw orthodox schools embrace theological liberalism. While the story is told adequately elsewhere,[24] the point of this paper is to show how this transition was felt between generations within a family of ministers in the United States.

A classic example of the transition from orthodoxy to liberalism in early Baptist life is Crawford Howell Toy (1836–1919).[25] Toy, a Virginia-born Southern Baptist, enrolled in the new Southern Baptist Theological Seminary of Greenville, South Carolina in its inaugural year.[26] Toy finished three quarters of the three year program in the first year and went on to Richmond College to teach Greek. At the same time, he prepared to go to Japan as a missionary. The War between the States broke out and he served as a chaplain, but was soon captured at Gettysburg and spent time in a Union prisoner of war camp, derailing missionary aspirations. Following the war he traveled to Germany where he studied Sanskrit and Semitics, sitting under men like Isaak A. Dorner (1809–84). Toy returned to the United States and began teaching first at Furman and then, a year later in 1869, at the new

---

24. For a sample of the discussion, see Jerry Wayne Brown, *The Rise of Biblical Criticism in America, 1800–1870* (Middletown, CT: Wesleyan University Press, 1969); Kenneth Cauthen, *The Impact of American Religious Liberalism* (New York: Harper and Row, 1962); Gary Dorrien, *The Making of American Liberal Theology—Imagining Progressive Religion 1805–1900* (Louisville: John Knox, 2001); Frank H. Foster, *The Modern Movement in American Theology. Sketches in the History of American Protestant Thought from the Civil War to the World War* (New York: Revell, 1939); William R. Hutchison, *The Modernist Impulse in American Protestantism* (Cambridge: Harvard University Press, 1976); *Liberal Protestantism*, edited by Bernard Reardon (Stanford: Stanford University Press, 1968). See also Jeffrey P. Straub, "The Making of a Battle Royal: The Rise of Theological Liberalism in Northern Baptist Life, 1870–1920" (PhD diss., Southern Baptist Theological Seminary, 2004).

25. Biographical information on Toy may be found in *Dictionary of American Religious Biography*, 559–60; *National Cyclopedia of American Biography*, 6:423; Dan Gentry Kent, "The Saint's Suitor: Crawford H. Toy," *Baptist History and Heritage* (Winter 2003) 6–16; Billy Grey Hurt, "Crawford Howell Toy: Interpreter of the Old Testament" (ThD diss., Southern Baptist Theological Seminary, 1965); David G. Lyon, "Crawford Howell Toy, 1836–1919," *Harvard Graduate Magazine*, 28 (December 1919) 266–69; David G. Lyon, "Crawford Howell Toy," *HTR* 13 (January 1920) 1–22; David G. Lyon et al., "Minute on the Life and Service of Professor Crawford Howell Toy," *Harvard University Gazette* (June 14, 1919) 128, 151–52. For a list of Toy's writings, see Hurt, "Crawford Howell Toy," 320–31.

26. For a new history of this institution, see Gregory A. Wills, *Southern Baptist Theological Seminary, 1859–2009* (New York: Oxford, 2009). The Toy affair can be found on 108–49.

Southern Baptist seminary. In a relatively orthodox inaugural address,[27] he pledged himself to the old orthodoxy (the orthodoxy of the founders James Petigru Boyce (1827–88) and John Albert Broadus (1827–95) and he acquitted himself of embracing the rationalism then flowing out of Germany. Nevertheless, he did not escape the German influence unscathed. He adopted a "mediating position" between the higher criticism and the old orthodoxy.[28] This would eventually move Toy from a position of perceived orthodoxy to sympathy with the new theology that was widely challenging the Protestant movement in America. The process started with Toy's questioning the inspiration and inerrancy of the Bible. He also adopted higher critical views on the authorship of the Pentateuch and related matters. The shift became deep and apparent among the students and faculty alike. It was also beginning to affect the churches.

By 1877 Toy's ideas appeared in print, first through one of his more zealous students, William C. Lindsay, pastor of the First Baptist Church of Columbia, South Carolina. He argued those views in the South Carolina Baptist paper, *The Working Christian*, under the pen name of Senex.[29] By 1878, Toy himself was openly espousing his views in print, in the pages of the *Sunday School Times*.[30]

Soon the matter became so public that the seminary board had to deal with the controversy by accepting Toy's resignation. He became the first "martyr" among modernism's rising host. Toy left Southern and eventually secured a position at the radically progressive Harvard Divinity School which acquiesced to liberalism seventy-five years earlier. There he remained for the rest of his life eventually leaving Baptist ranks altogether, falling in with the Unitarians. His influence continued to be felt among Baptists through his former students including David Gordon Lyon (1852–1935), a man who studied under Toy at Southern and left with him. Lyon became his colleague

---

27. See "The claims of Biblical interpretation on Baptists: being the inaugural address of Rev. C. H. Toy, on his induction into the professorship of Old Testament interpretation in Southern Baptist Theological Seminary, at Greenville, SC, September 1st, 1869" (Lange and Hilman, 1869).

28. See Wills, *Southern Baptist Theological Seminary*, 112–13, for details.

29. For instance, see "Letter to My Friend" nos. 1–4, *The Working Christian*, May 24, 1877; May 31, 1877; June 7, 1877; and June 14, 1877. All of these were signed simply "Senex."

30. The Toy articles appeared in "Critical Notes," *Sunday School Times*, April 12, 1878 and April 19, 1878. See also Pope A. Duncan, "Crawford Howell Toy: Heretic at Louisville," *American Religious Heretics*, ed. George H. Shriver (New York: Abingdon, 1966) 66.

at Harvard but remained active in Baptist life, speaking occasionally at national Baptist gatherings such as the Autumnal Conference.[31]

Not all those who embraced theological liberalism studied abroad and picked up their views overseas. Some men studied within the United States at places where theological liberalism had already attained hegemony by the mid-point in the nineteenth century. One such individual was Ezra Palmer Gould (1841–1900), who graduated from Harvard in 1861 and enrolled in Newton Theological Institution, following service in the Civil War.

Gould's teaching career at Newton began the same year that Alvah Hovey (1820–1903) commenced his thirty-year tenure as president. The presidency had been vacant at Newton since Barnas Sears (1802–80) stepped down twenty years earlier. Hovey set out to build the faculty by adding Heman Lincoln (1821–87), to teach Church History and Oakman Sprague Stearns (1822–81), to teach Biblical Literature and Interpretation in the Old Testament. With Stearns, the young Ezra Gould was jointly appointed to replace the widely-respected Horatio Balch Hackett (1808–75), long-time Professor of Biblical Literature and Interpretation. Hackett, along with fellow Newton professors Irah Chase (1793–1864) and Barnas Sears (1802–80), all studied in Germany during a time of radical theological turmoil.[32] Exactly how much of the new disposition was transplanted to

---

31. D. G. Lyon, "The Results of Modern Biblical Criticism," in the *Proceedings of the Second Annual Baptist Autumnal Conference* (Boston: Tremont Temple, 1883) 61–64. Also D. G. Lyon, "Are the Scriptures Free from Error?" in the *Proceedings of the Tenth Baptist Congress* (New York: Baptist Congress, 1892) 68–77. On Lyons, see Straub, "The Making of a Battle Royal," 87; Robert H. Pfeiffer, "David Gordon Lyon, 1852–1935," *Proceeding of the American Academy of Arts and Sciences* 70 (March 1936) 552–54, or George A. Barton, "David Gordon Lyon: in Memoriam," *Bulletin of the American Schools of Oriental Research* 62 (April 1936) 2–4.

32. Chase spent part of 1823–24 at the Universities of Halle and Göttingen, while Sears spent time with August Tholuck and Wilhelm Gesenius at Halle and with the faculty at Berlin during his European trip of 1833–35. For biographical information on Irah Chase, see Irah Chase, "Rev. Irah D. Chase, D. D.: An Autobiographical Sketch," *Baptist Memorial and Monthly Record* 9 (1850) 70–82; *General Catalogue of the Newton Theological Institution*, 24; Brackney, *HDB*, 97; *DAB*, 4:25–26; William Hague, *Life and Services of the Rev. Irah Chase* (Boston: Gould & Lincoln, 1866); *In Memoriam: A Tribute of Affection Professor Irah Chase* (Boston: Privately printed, 1865); Cathcart, *Baptist Encyclopedia*, 205–6; See also Brackney, *Genetic History*, 278–82. On Barnas Sears, consult Alvah Hovey, *Barnas Sears* (New York: Silver and Burdett, 1902); Brackney, *HDB*, 372–73. For a summary of Sears' studies in Germany, see Hovey, *Barnas Sears*, 35–53; and Brackney, *Genetic History*, 280–84. For a recent history of Newton, see Margaret Lamberts Bendroth, *A School of the Church: Andover Newton Across Two Centuries* (Grand Rapids: Eerdmans, 2008). Also consult William H. Brackney, *Congregation and*

American soil at Newton is difficult to determine. Irah Chase was exposed to progressive views during his brief visit to Germany but does not seem to have strayed too far from historic Baptist views at Newton. Certainly the installation of Hovey at Newton as president suggests that Newton was generally committed to the older orthodoxy and Hovey himself would be a regular champion of those views.[33]

Hackett was the only professor still teaching when Gould entered Newton in 1865.[34] In 1868, Hackett resigned his faculty appointment to devote himself to the work of the American Bible Revision Committee and Gould, his former student, was chosen to handle the New Testament classes. Though Gould had only recently graduated, Hovey had "the highest expectations, comparing him favorably with Doctor Hackett."[35] Evidently, Hovey's assessment proved true. "As an original thinker, as a master interpreter, laying hold of the fundamental thought of the sacred writer, and as a stimulating teacher, Professor Gould equaled his distinguished predecessor."[36] But Gould soon proved to be too progressive for Hovey and his views caused his departure from the faculty, but not before he left a lasting legacy in the lives of some of the students, especially on a pastor's son, William Herbert Perry Faunce.

Campus: North American Baptists in Higher Education (Macon: Mercer University Press, 2009) 260–62 and *passim*.

33. On Hovey and inspiration, see Straub, "The Making of a Battle Royal," 54–55, esp. n. 23.

34. On Hackett, see *Memorials of Horatio Balch Hackett*, ed. George H. Whittmore (Rochester: E. R. Andrews, 1876). Hackett's trip to Germany in 1841–42 took him to Halle to study under Gesenius and Tholuck and to Berlin to study under Hengstenberg and Neander, also hearing others when the occasion arose. See *Memorial of Horatio Balch Hackett*, 38–50. Norman Maring is doubtless correct when he suggested that "these three men [Chase, Sears and Hackett] did much to promote the scientific study of the Bible, the spirit of inquiry and the keen regard for truth with which many graduates were to be stamped." Norman Maring, "Baptists and Changing Views of the Bible, 1865–1918" Pt. 1, *Foundations* 1 (July 1958) 56.

35. George R. Hovey, *Alvah Hovey—His Life and Letters* (Philadelphia, 1928) 129. George Rice Hovey, the son of Alvah Hovey, grew up on the campus of Newton and likely had much firsthand knowledge of Alvah and his colleagues.

36. Hovey, *Alvah Hovey*, 168.

Departing from a Father's Faith: William Herbert Perry Faunce—A Case Study

Born into the home of Baptist clergyman Daniel Worcester Faunce in January of 1859, William was reared on older orthodoxy, then the common view of his day. The elder Faunce believed that God's inspiration came

> through good men to teach the world authoritatively the truth it needs to know. There is a human element; and so we see various styles and methods of writing. But there is, we claim, a divine element, and this overspreads and animates the human; the stronger using the weaker. As God is true, so his word is true. It is without admixture of error, and is thus the final authority in faith, in doctrine, in duty; and it contains all about religion that we need to know or can know on earth.[37]

In handling alleged errors of fact, such as in the realm of science, Daniel suggested that the Bible contained no scientific error. It merely employs the popular language of the day to speak to the issues but as such, "it teaches nothing about science."[38] At the same time he was adamant in affirming God's inspiration, he was most emphatic that the religious truths of the Bible are without error. If it bears human infelicities, these are of little concern. "These men are men; and it is *men* for whom we claim inspiration. But they are men used of God as the stronger uses the weaker; God's inspiration preserving them from error when they utter religious truth."[39]

Daniel also held to the miraculous in the Bible. To deny miracles required "the assumption that one is himself God!"[40] To argue that miracles are impossible because they are so highly improbable is also absurd.

> No one alleges miracles to be common; that, common, they would cease to be miracles. It is admitted at once, that they are not probable as every day occurrence. Nor is their commonness claimed. But only this; that at certain periods of time, when they were needed, God thrust in miracles for man's good.[41]

At the same time and typical of younger men of his era, Faunce embraced a non-literal approach to the creation story. In studying the first

---

37. Faunce, *A Young Man's Difficulties*, 71.
38. Faunce, *A Young Man's Difficulties*, 75.
39. Faunce, *A Young Man's Difficulties*, 83.
40. Faunce, *A Young Man's Difficulties*, 100.
41. Faunce, *A Young Man's Difficulties*, 100.

chapter of Genesis, "we must not forget that it does not fix *any time* for the creation of the matter out of which the earth was formed. . . . If the geologist can show proof that the creation occurred a thousand millions of years ago, Moses in the first two verses of Genesis does not contradict him."[42] Faunce argued that the Bible and science could be harmonized by a day-age theory and held that belief in six twenty-four-hour days was not necessary.[43] In this view, the elder Faunce was not far out of step with other orthodox men of his generation, including the Princetonians who made allowance for an evolutionary model within orthodoxy. Despite this one problem, Daniel W. Faunce seems to have espoused the old orthodoxy and passed that heritage along to his son.

After high school, William went on the study at Brown University of Providence, Rhode Island, where he earned the A. B. in 1880. Following Brown, he entered Newton Theological Institution to study for the ministry. Faunce graduated from Newton in 1884 and was ordained in June at the State Street Baptist of Springfield, Massachusetts. He served the State Street congregation for five years, until he received a call to the prestigious Fifth Avenue Baptist of New York.

After a prosperous ten-year ministry in New York, Faunce was offered the presidency of Brown University. He accepted and moved to Providence, Rhode Island, where he spent the remainder of his life, overseeing Brown's transition from a denominationally-oriented school to a major non-sectarian research university.[44] While president of Brown Faunce became a major object of the criticism of the fundamentalists for his liberal views.[45] The account

---

42. Emphasis in the original. Faunce, *A Young Man's Difficulties*, 126.

43. Faunce, *A Young Man's Difficulties*, 127.

44. It was during the Faunce presidency that Brown University removed its requirement that the president be a member of the Baptist clergy. Faunce's successor, Clarence Barbour, was also a Baptist clergyman, but Barbour's successor, Henry Merritt Wriston, eleventh president of Brown, became the first non-Baptist to hold the top job at Brown in its 173-year history. For a history of Brown University, see Reuben Guild, *Early History of Brown University and the Life and Times of James Manning* (n.p.: Snow and Farham, 1896); and Walter C. Bronson, *A History of Brown University* (Providence: Brown University, 1914). Also Janet M. Phillip, *Brown University, A Short History* (Providence: Brown University, 2000). Another excellent source on Brown is Martha Mitchell, *Encyclopedia Brunoniana* (Providence: Brown University, 1993). Mitchell was the long-time archivist until her retirement in 2003. Available at http://www.brown.edu/Administration/News_Bureau/Databases/Encyclopedia. Accessed November 16, 2009.

45. Biographical information on Faunce is plentiful. See *American National Biography*, 7:761–62; *DAB*, 3/2:299–301; Mitchell, *Encyclopedia Brunoniana*, 220–22; *Cyclopedia of Northern Baptist Ministers*, compiled by E. J. Brockett, Scrapbook "Do-G,"

of Faunce's personal journey to liberalism needs to be rehearsed at this point in the paper. It will serve as an example of the father/son angst that likely was repeated across numerous denominations during the rise of theological liberalism as the sons departed from the faith of their fathers.

Searching for Answers

During his youth, William struggled with his father's orthodoxy. His personal diary, as well as extant correspondence with his father, reveals a young man filled with doubts about his faith. While at Brown, he wrote to Daniel expressing certain reservations. William had read Huxley and Darwin and appreciated them, especially since certain religious teachers "derided" them. He was inclined more toward natural religion than revealed religion because doubters rejected his biblical arguments. He placed reason above revelation.

> After all, isn't man's own *reason* the final tribunal which must decide the matter? Some Christians say a man must not depend on his own reason, for that will lead him astray; but he must accept what the Bible says. But how shall he know the Bible is true, i. e. a *real revelation*, except by his reason. So that is not natural religion the first thing to be considered and then the Bible an auxiliary to it?[46]

Moreover, even the Bible itself left a confusing record. It was as much a source of heresy as truth. "Every creed in Christendom finds its support and foundation in the Bible. You and I are supposed to believe that our creed is the only one exactly true, and that all the other thousands are false. And all these heresies are based on a direct revelation from God!"[47]

Doubtless the older Faunce would have expected that young William's doubts would be alleviated while at Newton. The opposite actually

---

85–86; and J. Walter Sillen, "William H. Faunce, A Representative Religious Liberal," *Foundations* 2 (1959) 235–49. Faunce's personal papers (herein designated as WHPFP) are housed in the John Hay Library, Brown University, Providence, Rhode Island. No effort to further locate the documents herein cited from this collection will be made in this paper as the archives possesses a detailed finding aid which will make the location of the documents cited within the collection quite simple. A bibliography of Faunce's works is found at the end of Sillen, "William H. Faunce," 248–49.

46. W. H. Faunce to D. W. Faunce, March 9, 1879, WHPFP, John Hay Library, Brown University, Providence, Rhode Island. Emphasis occurs in the letter by underlining.

47. W. H. Faunce to D. W. Faunce, March 9, 1879.

occurred. William found his misgivings reinforced in the classroom. When Faunce attended Newton, Ezra Palmer Gould was creating a conflict over progressive views. Before his departure, Gould made a profound impression on young Faunce. "Gould is the best man I have yet met. He has practical common sense and is perfectly fearless—2 great essentials in a commentator. Learning is goo, [sic] but it often smothers mothers' wit. It has not been in Gould's case. It is a treat to hear him."[48] Faunce felt Gould was the best member of the faculty but considered transferring to Andover where there was more doctrinal openness. Instead, he spent a year at Brown, teaching mathematics (1881–82).

He returned to Newton to finish his seminary work, but not completely happy with the disposition of the school or with Alvah Hovey, its president. Gould had been forced to resign in 1882 under Hovey's commitment to orthodoxy. Faunce studied theology under Hovey, but resisted his views. In a letter to Daniel, William enquired about his father's view of an article on the atonement by Samuel Graves.[49] Graves argued that the primary issue for the atonement was God's love, not his wrath: "the Atonement is a revelation and a satisfaction of God's love for men, 'even the rebellious.'"[50] He furthermore asserted that no particular theory of the atonement was taught in the Bible.[51] He felt that the "penal-infliction" theory was unsatisfactory as an explanation for the atonement. "In what the Bible affirms respecting the sufferings of Christ human behalf it is nowhere said that he suffered *penally* for the guilt of man—that Christ was punished for our sins."[52] William expressed sympathy with Graves. "We students like it. Dr. Hovey labors hard to inculcate his view, but does not carry the seminary

---

48. William H. Faunce, personal journal, September 1880–1920, entry dated December 9, 1880, Brown University Archives, Providence, Rhode Island. Faunce was at this time struggling with his own theological perspective and was doubtless aided in his own journey toward liberalism by the influence of Ezra Gould.

49. Samuel Graves, "A Study of the Atonement," *Baptist Quarterly Review* 5 (1883) 193–218. Graves seems to have held this view for most of his academic career. See Samuel Graves, *Outlines of Theology* (Boston: C. H. Simonds, 1892) 57–67. Graves (1820–1905) graduated from Colgate Seminary 1846 and taught theology at Kalamazoo College (1851–59); was president of Atlanta Baptist Seminary (1885–90) and taught theology at Colgate (1890–94). On Graves, see *A General Catalogue of Colgate University, 1819–1919* (Hamilton: Colgate University Press, 1919) 13; and Cathcart, *Baptist Encyclopedia*, 468–69.

50. Graves, "A Study of the Atonement," 194.

51. Graves, "A Study of the Atonement," 195.

52. Graves, "A Study of the Atonement," 206.

with him. He insists on saying that Christ bore the *penalty* of our sins—and there I cannot follow him."[53]

The younger Faunce also defended to his father a young Baptist progressive named Philip S. Moxom. (1848–1923)[54] Moxom, pastor of First Baptist Church of Cleveland, had written an article for the *Standard* in support of the "new theology." William was guarded but supportive of Moxom's views.

> I fear you and I will never agree here. I think he has done a most foolish thing in rushing into print. He who spends his youth in getting into print, may spend his age in trying to get out of it. But with his sentiments I am in sympathy. The only difference between him and a hundred others is that he *speaks* and others *think*. I would not use perhaps his expression, certainly if I did, I would insist also on the other side of the matter. I think his mistake is in his *omissions*, not his assertions. Every assertion that he makes, I think I agree with. But his mistake—see a most judicious editorial in the Standard—is in not bringing out also certain other truths which do not *contradict* but *counterbalance* the first.[55]

William came to question the Bible's inspiration.

> Dr. Crane of Boston says that scripture is inspired only in a higher degree than Plato—certainly I would not say that. But let me, father, build my own theological tower—I have only just begun to build—"foursquare to all the winds that blow." Let me try the spirits, whether they be of God. Let me be in hearty earnest sympathy with my age, with every movement of thought within and without the church, and do not fear that I shall be a castaway.[56]

53. W. H. Faunce to D. W. Faunce, April 25, 1883, WHPFP.

54. Philip Stafford Moxom (1848–1923), a Canadian-born Baptist, graduated from Rochester Seminary in 1878. He was a prominent pastor and advocate of the liberal agenda. He pastored First Baptist of Cleveland, Ohio, and later First Baptist of Boston. He left the Baptist ranks to pastor the South Congregational Church of Springfield, Massachusetts. The official chronicler of First Baptist, Boston, noted that significant differences "intensified" over time resulting in his separation from the assembly without specifying the nature of those problems. See Nathan Wood, *The History of First Baptist Church of Boston* (Philadelphia: ABPS, 1899) 345–46.

55. W. H. Faunce to D. W. Faunce, incomplete letter, circa 1883, WHPFP. Moxom's article was "A New Theology: A Contribution to Progressive Christian Orthodoxy," *The Standard*, August 23, 1883. The article was reprinted as Philip S. Moxom, *A New Theology* (Philadelphia: Samuel Loag, n.d.).

56. W. H. Faunce to D. W. Faunce, incomplete letter, circa 1884, WHPFP. Cephas B. Crane (1833–1917) was pastor of First Baptist Church of Boston (1878–84) and member

As William came to the end of his Newton journey, he considered his options. Among them was a study trip to Germany. However, his father seems to have argued against this possibility because of William's manifest proclivities. About this time, William made the following entry into his personal journal.

> I live on a floating island. I have gone just far enough to stir up the sediment of my mind, now it must take time to settle and crystallize. Atonement, justification, incarnation, eternal punishment—about these central truths I am all afloat.... I feel the influence of (the) new theology—Andover and Newman Smyth are a power in our present tht [sic] [thought?] and I eagerly read their utterances. Not that I follow them, but I am watching them. The Xian Union and Independent are to me a weekly feast (of) fat things. Our Baptist papers are generally crabbed and narrow. My mind is full of unanswered questions.[57]

Into the Ministry

Given the direction of William's thinking as he matured and his father's commitment to orthodoxy, it seems more than coincidental at this point that the elder's books dealt directly or indirectly with the issues with which William was wrestling. They seemed to parallel the correspondence between father and son. The titles themselves may give an insight into what Daniel attempted to do in encouraging his son to remain within the bounds of orthodoxy. These latter books appear in print as William's liberalism becomes more pronounced and public.

After graduation from Newton, William was called to the pastorate of the State Street Baptist Church of Springfield, MA. It was the church in which he served while a student. His father preached the charge to the candidate, and Ezekiel G. Robinson (1815–94),[58] the ordination sermon.

---

of the trustee committee that investigated the orthodoxy of Gould.

57. William H. Faunce, Personal Journal, 1880–1920, 233,WHPFP.

58. Robinson had been the president of Rochester Theological Seminary and its professor of systematic theology. He went on to serve as president of Brown University from 1872–89. Two of his most prominent students were his successor at Rochester, A. H. Strong and Faunce. For more on Robinson see, *Ezekiel Gilman Robinson* (Boston: Silver & Burdett, 1896); Brackney, *HDB*, 353–54; Brackney, *A Genetic History of Baptist Thought* (Macon: Mercer University Press, 2004) 318–25; N. H. Maring, "Robinson, Ezekiel Gilman, 1815-1894," *DBA*, 238; James Leo Garrett, *Baptist Theology—A Four*

Once for All Delivered to the Saints

His youthful heterodox drift continued following graduation. For example, he utterly rejected A. H. Strong's Augustinianism as

> radically false, absurd and abhorrent. . . . How any human being could ever hold in any real true sense that "in Adam's fall we sinned all." I not only regret the dogma, but I declare eternal enmity to it, it is my intention to fight the wretched theological fiction as long as I live. I believe Paul's word rightly interpreted means no such thing.[59]

He sided with the Andover progressives,[60] and continued to align himself with the theology of Philip Moxom. His view of inspiration was "*human, rational, worthy*, I would say. I teach my young men that the flood was only partial though the writer of Genesis thought it universal. I teach that the scripture account of creation is purely religious."[61]

During these years, Daniel continued to address theological issues typically challenged by liberalism. His next published book concerned the resurrection and was dedicated in the memory of Fred W. Faunce, a young son who had died at the age of twelve. In this volume, Faunce affirmed the orthodox view of the resurrection from the dead because of the resurrection of Jesus. For Daniel, belief in Christ's resurrection was the ground upon which the truth of Christianity rested. "Our whole system of faith is swept by the board if that fact be taken from us. Everything falters if that be doubtful."[62]

The State Street church would not long keep young William. His pulpit eloquence and demeanor soon caught the eye of the search committee of the prestigious Fifth Avenue Baptist Church of New York City. Among its regular attenders were the Rockefellers—John Davison Sr., founder of Standard Oil and one of the wealthiest men in America, and his brother William Rockefeller, a member of the board of Standard Oil and nearly as

---

Century Study (Macon: Mercer University Press, 2009) 288–91.

59. W. H. Faunce to D. W. Faunce, January 24, 1887, WHPFP.

60. Andover Seminary had been started in 1807 in response to the theological capture of Harvard by the Unitarians. However, within a few years, Andover too succumbed to the spirit of the age and embraced liberalism. For a brief history of this, see Daniel Day Williams, *The Andover Liberals: A Study in American Theology* (originally published in 1940; New York: Octagon Books, 1970).

61. W. H. Faunce to D. W. Faunce, January 24, 1887, WHPFP. Emphasis in the original.

62. See D. W. Faunce, *Resurrection in Nature and Revelation: An Argument and a Meditation* (New York: Anson D. F. Randolph, 1884).

wealthy as his older brother. Faunce's ministry at Fifth Avenue commenced in 1889 and lasted ten years. Both he and the church prospered during his New York days. William received invitations to serve as a guest lecturer at the University of Chicago in homiletics, 1897–98, and from Harvard to serve as the resident preacher, 1898–99. During this time, he would turn the historic church in a new direction.[63]

By the time William became the pastor of the Fifth Avenue, he was a committed liberal. He remained so to the end of his days, promoting the liberal agenda wherever he could. The church, however, was still inclined toward the older orthodoxy. That posture would change under Faunce's ministry. By the time he resigned in just ten short years, Fifth Avenue was firmly committed to the liberal ethos and would go on to become one of the most prominent liberal pulpits not only among the Baptists but across America under the progressive leadership of Harry Emerson Fosdick (1878–1969).[64]

> "He [Faunce] fed us liberal fare without our knowing it," recalled one church member years later, and this change of diet was soon having a refreshing effect upon the church. "Gradually," another member recorded, "there disappeared from official records the piety in expression which up to that time characterized the language of most Protestant churches."[65]

William's mature view of the Bible may be found in an address he delivered numerous times starting in 1898.[66] Taking as his text Ps 119:16,

---

63. Faunce entered the pastorate at Fifth Avenue in 1889, succeeding the illustrious Thomas Armitage who had pastored the church for forty years. On Armitage, see Cathcart, *Baptist Encyclopedia*, 39–41; H. L. McBeth, "Armitage, Thomas (1819–1896)," *DBA*, 32; Brackney, *HDB*, 26; *Services Commemorative of the Close of Forty Years of Pastoral Service under Thomas Armitage, D. D., L.L.D.* (n.p.: n.p., 1888).

64. Biographical data on Fosdick may be found in Brackney, *The Baptists*, 167–68; Brackney, *HDB*, 64–65; *DBA*, s.v. "Fosdick, Harry Emerson," by C. W. Whiteman, 120–21. Also important is Fosdick's autobiography, Harry Emerson Fosdick, *The Living of These Days* (New York: Harper, 1956). In recent years two important works on Fosdick have been written. The first is a important biography by Robert Moats Miller, *Harry Emerson Fosdick* (New York: Oxford University Press, 1985). Also very helpful is a dissertation by Henry E. Ernst, *American Protestant Liberalism as Exemplified in the Life and Thought of Harry Emerson Fosdick* (PhD diss., St. Mary's Seminary and University, 1988).

65. Mina Pendo, *A Brief History of the Riverside Church* (n.p.: Riverside Church, 1957) 27.

66. The address "How Much Is Left?" was delivered at least seven times, including at Harvard in January 1899; Chautauqua in 1899; Brown in 1900; Cornell in 1900; and

he posed a question he had been asked repeatedly concerning the Bible—"How much is left?" First, he argued, "The idea (of the) Bible as a single book, miraculously produced and preserved is gone forever. . . . The Bible did not drop out of the sky at some miraculous moment. It grew by slow accretion and every page bears (the) imprint (of) its time."[67] Second, "the idea (of the) Bible as scientifically and historically inerrant has gone forever. Of course the Bible never made any such claim for itself, but our unbelieving and fearsome theology has often made that claim on its behalf." The Bible was not meant to teach science, but life; a "pedantic accuracy is beside the mark."[68] Third, "the idea, therefore, that this library [is of] equal value in all its parts is gone forever. The Bible is nowhere [in the] scripture called [the] Word [of] God. That title is applied to X. [Christ]"[69]

Daniel was no doubt concerned by the kinds of views expressed by William. While the historical record does give the full picture, perhaps the books that Daniel continued to write may shed some light on the issues of concern. Daniel penned two books that addressed issues identified with liberalism during William's Fifth Avenue years.

In 1892, three years after William assumed the pulpit at New York, Daniel wrote *Letters to a Skeptic*. Its format was "imaginary conversations" with a skeptic. Daniel hoped that God would "use it in guiding some struggling soul through perplexity into faith."[70] Among the topics addressed was the atonement, long a source of concern for William. Regarding the atonement, the older orthodoxy held that the death of Christ actually paid a penalty for sin. William, nevertheless, had rejected that categorically in response to the teaching of Alvah Hovey. As noted above, he was more inclined toward the view expressing the atonement as an ethical atonement.

According to this view of the atonement, its result as applied to the redeemed is not, in its inner nature, a legal process, so that they are pronounced just, nor a commercial process, or the mere payment of their debts—though both may be used as illustrations of grace as far as they go,—but an ethical transaction in which, by the manifested love and holiness of God in Christ, coming forth in time to save the sinner by taking upon himself through loving sympathy the consequences and costs of our

---

Johns Hopkins in 1900.

67. "How Much Is Left," 4–5.
68. "How Much Is Left," 7–8.
69. "How Much Is Left," 10.
70. D. W. Faunce, *Hours with a Skeptic*, "Prefatory Note."

sin, and so stamping his eternal condemnation of sin, the enmity and alienation of the human heart is removed and "we are reconciled to God by the death of His Son," i.e., there takes the place of enmity in our hearts love and trust—i.e., ethical as contrasted with legal justification.[71]

To this view, William, who was in attendance when the above quote was uttered, was in full sympathy.

> Mr. President:—At this time of night it would be unpardonable for us to prolong this discussion, but I cannot go to the hospitable home which awaits me without saying how proud I am of being a member of a Congress which can produce three such papers as we have enjoyed this evening. They show us that our young men are grappling with the great problems of the faith; they show us that they believe in more than mere emotionalism in religion....
>
> We are growing dissatisfied with all merely commercial theories, all analogies from book-keeping and the multiplication table. We feel sure that what Christ did for us must be something that summons us onward as with a bugle-call. What is true of Him is true in lesser degree of all his disciples. Did He die for men? "Like as Christ laid down his life for us, so ought we to lay down our lives for the brethren." Is He now above all glory raised? Still He prays that "Where I am, ye may be also." Unitarianism is reducing Christ to the level of men. Evangelicalism consists in lifting men to the level of Christ, viewing Him as the norm and goal of humanity.
>
> Thus we are finding the atonement more human, more real, more truly a shaping power in daily life.[72]

Still Daniel labored to convince his readers (and perhaps his own son) that more than this was involved in the atonement. It was a penal transaction. Daniel spoke in terms of how much we owed God for sin. "Penalty is certainly owed to the law, and if penalty for sin is to be escaped there must be reparation of some sort."[73] "I want to enter a claim in behalf of Christianity that we have here a most unique presentation. We have a substituted person who is a unique character, and also a substituted sorrow for the penalty of sin."[74]

---

71. R. G. Boville, "Ethical versus Forensic Conceptions of Salvation," *Proceedings of the Eleventh Baptist Congress held at Augusta, GA, December 1893* (New York: Baptist Congress Publishing, 1894) 66.

72. See comments by William H. Faunce in *Proceedings of the Eleventh Baptist Congress*, 74.

73. Faunce in *Proceedings of the Eleventh Baptist Congress*, 152.

74. Faunce in *Proceedings of the Eleventh Baptist Congress*, 160.

Several years later, Daniel took up again the matter of inspiration in a monograph study which he dedicated to William, though it expressed views that William had long since given up. Daniel believed in a form of inerrancy without surrendering the human element. "The divine element is needed to correct the human."[75] "Man's book has God's superintendence in all its parts."[76] Yet, he seems to have limited inerrancy to the religious elements.[77] But still, the divine element in the Bible was needed to correct the human. The divine element included four aspects—"the selection of the writers," "their instruction in the subject-matter of their writings," "the guidance of the Spirit in the selection of the words employed by the sacred writers," and "the absolute truth of all things written."[78] This was far more than William was willing to concede.

A Mature Man and His Bible

William ended his pastoral career in 1899 when he was invited to assume the presidency of Brown University of Providence, Rhode Island. Brown was the "mother" of Baptist education in America, having been formed by the Philadelphia Association in 1764 as the College of Rhode Island. It had a long history of illustrious Baptist clergymen who served as president and though it opened its doors to non-Baptists, at the time William went to Brown it was still largely under the control of the Baptists. About the time William moved to Brown, his father Daniel was nearing the end of his pastoral career. His final charge was at the Baptist Church at Pawtucket, RI, a few miles north of Providence. He retired in 1899 and joined his son in membership at First Baptist, Providence.[79] During his retirement, he continued to write. One final book, written three years before his death, may have been a last attempt to persuade William of some of the old orthodoxy. While William was questioning what was left of the Bible under the scrutiny

---

75 D. W. Faunce, *Inspiration Considered as a Trend*, 191.

76. Faunce, *Inspiration Considered as a Trend*, 193.

77. Faunce, *Inspiration Considered as a Trend*, 77–91.

78. Faunce, *Inspiration Considered as a Trend*, 200–201.

79. At his retirement, Daniel, along with his wife Mary, joined the First Baptist Church of Providence, Rhode Island, where he remained the rest of his life. His son, W. H. P. Faunce, and his wife, Sarah, joined the church the same day (December 26, 1899), William having relocated to Providence to assume the presidency of Brown University. See Henry M. King, *Historical Catalogue of the Members of First Baptist Church* (Providence, RI: F. H. Townsend, printer, 1908) 111.

of modern belief, Daniel was affirming its trustworthiness and importance. *A Mature Man's Difficulties with His Bible* continued to address the themes of his earlier works and persisted in displaying Daniel's commitment to a form of older orthodoxy. For Daniel, the Bible remained a divine book whose ultimate source was God. "The Bible purports to be God's history of God as he manifested himself, and as he has secured, through man, a record of those manifestations."[80] Inspiration was again defended, yet no one view was entirely satisfactory.[81] The Bible was more than a record of man's religious history; it was a history of "God's historic revelations of himself."[82] While he argued for the "accuracy in the teaching of moral fact and truth," he wanted the Bible to be allowed to "speak out for itself." We must be willing to "submit our opinion to it as the ultimate authority."[83] For William, what value was the Bible? It was a "Bible of experience" of spiritual pilgrims. Its value was to be measured by its religious effect on people. "The real testing has been done not (in a) critical seminar, but (in a) broad field (of) human history, not by any German scissors, but by (the) fact that the generations have come (to the) scripture for light and inspiration and peace and have not come in vain."[84] The Bible had little to do with one's faith. "A religious faith which depends absolutely on a doubtful reading in an ancient manuscript, a faith which is bound up with the question of whether a fish could swallow a man, or whether dead men actually rose and walked about in Jerusalem at the time of our Lord's crucifixion—such a faith is necessarily contingent, uncertain, timorous."[85]

William, despite his father's lifelong pleading, never turned from his liberal direction but only became more committed to it as the years went by. In an article in *World's Work*, May 1923, Faunce declared himself on the fundamentals of Christianity, then debated among Northern Baptists. He held evolution to be a firmly established fact and "one of the most powerful

---

80. D. W. Faunce, *A Mature Man's Difficulties*, 20.

81. Faunce, *A Mature Man's Difficulties*, 38.

82. Faunce, *A Mature Man's Difficulties*, 113.

83. Faunce, *A Mature Man's Difficulties*, 48–49.

84. "How Much Is Left?" 12, 18–19. Faunce delivered this message at Brown in 1900, early in his presidency. See also W. H. P. Faunce, "What Is the Use of the Bible?" An address delivered at Colorado College, December 1915; at the University of Chicago in January 1916; at Columbia University, in February 1916; at First Baptist Church of Providence, Rhode Island, November 1916; at Lake Mohonk, in August 1924; and again at First Baptist Church, Providence, in October, 1924, WHPFP.

85. W. H. P. Faunce, *What Does Christianity Mean?* (New York: Revell, 1912) 34.

aids to religious faith." He denied the inerrancy of the Bible, and by implication, he cast doubt about the Virgin Birth.

> The writer of the New Testament never ascribed inerrancy to the Old Testament, but on the contrary often pronounced its teaching defective and preparatory to something better. The Virgin birth, which is related with noble reticence and reverence in two New Testament passages and which has for centuries been accepted by the great majority of the church, is not mentioned in any New Testament epistle or in any of the apostolic sermons recorded in the Book of Acts.[86]

It is little wonder that by the time of the fundamentalist-modernist controversy, W. H. P. Faunce was identified as one of the most prominent of the Baptist liberals. He was repeatedly singled out by the conservatives as an example of the seriousness of the problem that plagued Northern Baptist education. In 1922, Charles Hillman Fountain published a lengthy critique of Faunce's book, *What Does Christianity Mean?*[87] In May of 1923, New York pastor John Roach Straton (1875–1929), boisterously objected to Faunce's appearance on the platform of the convention's annual meeting.[88] Later that year, Canadian Baptist T. T. Shields raised a loud protest when Faunce was given an honorary Doctor of Laws by McMaster University.[89]

---

86. W. H. P. Faunce, "The Fundamentals," *The World's Work*, May 1923 (reprinted in pamphlet form, Boston: Pilgrim, 1923) 8–9, 16. Also in an address delivered at the Mohonk conference first in 1924 on the Apostle's Creed, he would declare "the emphasis is not on (the) word 'Virgin' but (on) the words 'Mary' and 'born.' Our attitude toward (the) Virgin Birth depends on our reading (of the) NT. We may insist upon it as did Matthew and Luke; or we may ignore it, as did all (of the) apostles in their early preaching and all (of the) epistles (in the) NT." See William H. P. Faunce, "What Is the Use of the Apostle's Creed?" WHPFP.

87. Charles Hillman Fountain, *Charges of Teaching False Doctrine Are Herein Brought Against The Rev. William H. P. Faunce and The Rev. Gerald Birney Smith* (Plainfield, NJ: by the author, 1922).

88. "Dr. Straton Stirs Baptist Assembly," *Boston Herald*, May 24, 1923. Also "Baptists Shout Down Dr. Straton in Convention," *Philadelphia North American*, May 24, 1923. Cf. John Roach Straton, "Why I Object to the Appearance of Dr. W. H. P. Faunce to Deliver the Keynote Address at the Northern Baptist Convention," *The Fundamentalist*, June 1923, 3–4.

89. "McMaster Senate Disapproves Stand of Rev. Dr. Shields," *Toronto Globe*, January 15, 1924, 1. The degree was conferred on Faunce at the installation of Henry P. Whidden as Chancellor of McMaster. Also receiving honorary degrees at the November 12, 1923 meeting were George Edwin Horr of Newton and Edgar Y. Mullins of Southern Baptist Theological Seminary in Louisville, both of whom received a DMin degree.

William Herbert Perry Faunce was an unapologetic liberal and he was in the eye of the storm. It was a conflict that rent major American denominations and left in its wake division and chaos. Furthermore, William was not alone. He was in the company of many confederates, some of them sons of orthodox clergymen, who like him, had been raised in an older orthodoxy, only to reject that heritage for the new theology. How many other young men followed the pathway that William trod is impossible to determine. Clearly there were others—ministers whose sons and grandsons were raised according to the prevailing orthodox views of the early nineteenth century only to abandon those views by the end of that century.[90] The new theology had broken through and liberalism attained hegemony in American theology. As one surveys the landscape of American church history during the late nineteenth and early twentieth century, one wonders how many others like William began with *A Young Man's Difficulties with His Bible* and ended their pilgrimage by abandoning their father's faith.

---

90. Another ministerial father and son pair that may shed light on this transition is Nathan Smith Burton (1821–1909) and his son Ernest Dewitt Burton (1856–1925). Nathan, originally of Manlius, New York, graduated from Western Case Reserve College in 1846 and attended its theological school for one year and then studied for another year at Newton. He went on to pastor Baptist churches in Ohio, Michigan, Iowa, and Massachusetts. He also taught for a year and a half at Kalamazoo College (Jan. 1876–July 1877) and served for a year as acting president of Denison University in 1886, both of them Baptist institutions. Biographical information of Nathan may be found in Cathcart, *Baptist Encyclopedia*, 170, and in *General Catalogue of Newton*, 69. Ernest Dewitt Burton taught in the field of New Testament, first at Rochester (1882–83), from which he graduated in 1882, then at Newton (1883–92), and finally at the University of Chicago, where he eventually served as president. Biographical information on Ernest Dewitt Burton may be found in Thomas W. Goodspeed, *Ernest De Witt Burton: A Biographical Sketch* (Chicago: University of Chicago Press, 1926); Goodspeed, "Ernest De Witt Burton: His Larger Life," *University of Chicago Record* 12 (1926) 132–63; Brackney, *HDB*, 82; *DBA*, 68; *Denison University, 1831–1906*, 221; *Rochester General Catalogue, 1920*, 143; *General Catalogue of Newton, 1943*, 26; and *DAB* 2:341–42. Also "Ernest De Witt Burton," *Journal of Biblical Literature* 45 (1926) v–vi. Ernest Dewitt Burton was a key member of the faculty and administration of the prominently liberal University of Chicago in its early years. On his theology, see Straub, "The Making of a Battle Royal," 245–49. Ernest Dewitt publicly deviated from his father's orthodox view of inerrancy. See Ernest D. Burton, "A Few Words to Dr. Conant," *The Baptist*, November 4, 1922, 1244.

7

George Burman Foster

First Radical of the Chicago School

VAN E. CARPENTER

Introduction

RADICAL BEST DEFINES THE Chicago School, and George Burman Foster initiated the University of Chicago's Divinity School into the identity that coincides with this definition.[1] While neither the first nor the most fa-

---

1. It has been my distinct pleasure to have had many good discussions with Dr. Priest when he has visited his son and family (his son serves with me at Northland), and I hope to enjoy more of these conversations in the future. Dr. Priest and I share a common area of interest in the history of the fundamentalist-modernist controversy, and he is a reliable source of advice and encouragement in my own research.

The "Chicago School" is a recognized term with a rather loose meaning. In its usage here, I am referring to the school of thought promoted by theologians, philosophers, and social scientists of the University of Chicago during the first fifty years of the twentieth century. It was marked by a radicalism that embraced the sociohistorical methods of biblical research and the pragmatism of Ames and Dewey. Because historians of the affected disciplines debate the parameters of the Chicago School, Foster's involvement in and influence of that school remain part of the debate. More information may be found in Gragg (Alan Wayne Gragg, "Formative Influences on the Development of the Religious Humanism of George Burman Foster," PhD diss. [Durham, SC: Duke University, 1961] iii), Axel (Larry E. Axel, "God or Man at Chicago: The 'Chicago School' of Theology, with Special Reference to the Issue of Antecedents and to the Roles of G. B. Foster, E. S. Ames, and H. N. Wieman," PhD diss. [Philadelphia: Temple University, 1975] 175–76), Arnold (Charles Harvey Arnold, *Near the Edge of Battle: A Short History of the Divinity School*

mous of all of the theologians from the University of Chicago be they tenured or graduated, Foster remains the starting point for speaking of that institution's reputation as the home of Midwestern religious radicalism. He was a seminal influence upon Shailer Mathews, Gerald Birney Smith, George Cross, D. C. Macintosh, A. Eustace Hayden, and Curtis W. Reese. The first published theologian of Harper's fledgling university, the first Northern Baptist liberal to be "tried" for heresy and disfellowshipped from the Chicago Ministers' Conference, and the first Northern Baptist seminary professor to have his tenure moved from a divinity school to more favorable ground. Foster, with his pragmatic religious humanism, would provide the impetus for the development of several iterations and successions of increasingly radical theology.

This article will give a brief sketch of Foster's early life and subsequent education. Special consideration will be given to how early his radical tendencies seem to emerge. Later in the article, an outline and commentary on his career and some of the controversy surrounding his career will be presented. Finally, this article will offer an explanation and commentary on his theology. The article will tread lightly in the area of criticism in order to expound more fully a reasonable understanding of the effects of Foster's *curriculum vitae* upon theological scholarship.

Foster's Early Biography and Career

Early Life

George Burman Foster's life began in the home of a common laborer in Alderson, West Virginia on April 2, 1857. Much of the biography of Foster's early life may be found summarized briefly by a number of biographers, but most of the information contained here was derived by the earliest posthumous evaluation of the theological contribution of Foster by H. W. Johnson.[2] This information can be corroborated by a few primary sources, but Johnson's work remains the standard for Foster's biographical material. Johnson describes a laborer's home in which Foster's father, Oliver Har-

---

and the "Chicago School of Theology" 1866–1966 [Chicago: The Divinity School Association, The University of Chicago, 1966] 23–28), and Hynes (William J. Hynes, *Shirley Jackson Case and the Chicago School: The Socio-Historical Method*, Biblical Scholarship in North America: Society of Biblical Literature [Ann Arbor, MI: Scholars, 1981] 12).

2. Hjalmar Wilhelm Johnson, "The Religious Thought of George B. Foster," PhD diss. (St. Peter, MN: Yale University Press, 1931).

rison Foster, read the Bible, weekly papers and *The Journal and Messenger*.[3] Foster's mother "would have accepted the Bible as infallible beyond a doubt. The Bible in those days was generally accepted as being infallible.... [sic] The doubt of a single passage would have thrown the whole book into discard—it was all true or none at all."[4]

Education

Foster had a fondness for reading and a loathing of physical labor. At the age of sixteen, young Foster was "given his time" and began his formal education at Second Creek, West Virginia.[5] He would later enroll in Shelton College of St. Albans, West Virginia.[6] Dr. Powell Benton Reynolds (1841–1919) was revered by Foster as his "first great teacher."[7] Reynolds seems to have been conservative, but Johnson quotes another source who says "[Reynolds] was considered by religious bodies as a Fundamentalist, but at heart he was liberal for his day. He never preached or taught liberal views."[8]

In 1880, Foster enrolled at West Virginia University of Morgantown.[9] His performance there was such that he did well in humanities but not so well in science.[10] He was a Baptist preacher during this time and supported

---

3. Johnson, "The Religious Thought of George B. Foster," 120. This was a conservative paper. Straub has identified its editor as a proto-fundamentalist in his article: (Jeffrey P. Straub, "George William Lasher—Baptist Proto-Fundamentalist," *Detroit Baptist Seminary Journal* 11 [2006] 135–50).

4. These accounts of Foster's early life are replete with citations to letters from family members and acquaintances of Foster's. Lacking the ability to interview directly, letters of inquiry were sent out and people responded. These letters are all fastidiously cited. (Winifred Foster Skaggs, to Hjalmar Wilhelm Johnson, September 23, 1930; quoted in Johnson, "The Religious Thought of George B. Foster," 115–16n1).

5. Johnson, "The Religious Thought of George B. Foster," 123. See also the address of James Hayden Tufts in University of Chicago, "George Burman Foster: A Memorial Service at the University of Chicago," reprinted from *The University Record*, *The University Record* 5, no. 2 (April 1919) 180–85.

6. Johnson, "The Religious Thought of George B. Foster," 128. In footnote 2 of the same page, it is noted that the board of directors was composed entirely of Baptist preachers.

7. Johnson, "The Religious Thought of George B. Foster," 128.

8. Mabel Reynolds Glasscock to Hjalmar Wilhelm Johnson, November 25, 1930, quoted in Johnson, "The Religious Thought of George B. Foster," 130n4.

9. Johnson, "The Religious Thought of George B. Foster," 136–37.

10. Johnson, "The Religious Thought of George B. Foster," 141–42.

himself that way.¹¹ His university friend, McCutcheon, had this recollection in 1930:

> In those early days he was predominantly evangelistic. He conducted a number of revivals, as we called them, and was persuasive and powerful in his appeals to the unsaved. . . . Personally I detected no liberalism at all. But you must remember that was nearly fifty years ago, and I was young and inexperienced and could not have known what liberalism was. I do not recall any talk along this line by either students or professors.¹²

Foster received his AB degree in 1883 and married Mary Lyon, a daughter of one of his professors.¹³ During his junior year at West Virginia University he became the associate pastor of Morgantown Baptist Church under O. M. Miller. He would later become its senior pastor.¹⁴

Dr. D. B. Purinton, president emeritus of West Virginia University and member of Morgantown Baptist Church while Foster was pastoring there had this to say of his young pastor:

> In religious matters . . . [Foster was while at Morgantown] *progressive but conservative,* and, so far as I know, until he went to Germany, was considered *"orthodox"* even by the conservatives of that day.¹⁵

In another letter Purinton had this to say: "Foster and I were members of the same church and had frequent discussions on religious questions. We both believed in Evolution, and likewise the Personality of God, the Deity of Christ and his Vicarious Atonement."¹⁶ Purinton also stated that Foster "was one of the finest students [he] ever had, and was exceptionally thoughtful

---

11. Johnson, "The Religious Thought of George B. Foster," 142.

12. J. L. McCutcheon to Hjalmar Wilhelm Johnson, November 18, 1930, quoted in Johnson, "The Religious Thought of George B. Foster," 142–43n1.

13. Johnson, "The Religious Thought of George B. Foster," 143.

14. Johnson, "The Religious Thought of George B. Foster," 144–45.

15. D. B. Purinton to Hjalmar Wilhelm Johnson, August 5, 1930, quoted in Johnson, "The Religious Thought of George B. Foster," 145–46n1. Underscoring Johnson's.

16. D. B. Purinton to Hjalmar Wilhem Johnson, September 8, 1930, quoted in Johnson, "The Religious Thought of George B. Foster," 146n2. This was not an uncommon position among theologians of the day. The eminent A. H. Strong, who later taught Foster at Rochester, held similar views.

and able to think things through in an exhaustive analytical and logical fashion which is not often found among undergraduate students."[17]

Johnson has a personal recollection of Dr. D. C. Macintosh telling of Foster replying to his detractors "It is I who am the true conservative." However, his desire extended only to the conservation of the essential, allowing for reconstruction when it seemed implausible to do otherwise.[18]

Career

Rochester Divinity School

In 1884–85, when Foster was attending the Rochester Divinity School, he would have studied under A. H. Strong, Howard Osgood, William Arnold Stevens, T. Harwood Pattison, Benjamin O. True, Henry E. Robins, Adelbert S. Coats, Augustus Rauschenbusch, Herman M. Schaffer, Jacob S. Gubelmann, Gustav Ebmeyer, and Louis Vogt. Johnson remarks that all were conservative. He also indicates that the term *conservative* may also be applied to fundamentalists.[19] Johnson uses *fundamentalism* as a subset of *conservative*.

Johnson solicited several former classmates concerning Foster's questions during Strong's lectures and his reactions to the same. Some noted that he asked a good many questions. One student noted that he thought some of the questions were unnecessary. None recalled any major disagreements between the views of Foster then and Strong.[20] One former classmate made an extensive and generous observation of Foster during those years at Rochester:

While in the Seminary and at graduation Foster was regarded by all of us as one of Dr. Strong's foremost champions. He was a master of Dr. Strong's textbook on Theology and so far as we know he endorsed it in full and certainly conformed his preaching to its teachings.[21]

---

17. D. B. Purinton to Hjalmar Wilhelm Johnson, August 5, 1930, quoted in Johnson, "The Religious Thought of George B. Foster," 146n1.

18. Johnson, "The Religious Thought of George B. Foster," 149.

19. Johnson, "The Religious Thought of George B. Foster," 151–52.

20. Johnson, "The Religious Thought of George B. Foster," 227–30.

21. W. C. Taylor to Hjalmar Wilhelm Johnson, August 11, 1930, quoted in Johnson, "The Religious Thought of George B. Foster," 230–32n2.

At the end of the quote, he notes that Foster spurred his classmates on to preach "in all its loveliness, the old gospel."[22]

D. T. Denman's testimony, however, gives witness to what might be the first modernist impulse of Foster at this time:

> He had little disposition to keep in line with traditional views and assumed his right to come to his own conclusions. He was not disposed to accept the idea that religion was based upon a specific revelation, but held that philosophy and psychology had a contribution to make. His attitude in the seminary was in perfect harmony with his later ideas. There he was the later Foster in embryo. He was evidently the truth seeker. He was not skeptical, nor was he controversial. He was spiritually minded and possessed a remarkably sweet disposition. He was human and sympathetic to a fault. He was deeply admired and loved by all the students and was by far the outstanding intellect among the students of the seminary.[23]

In many of the letters included in Johnson's research, it is evident from the answers given that Johnson asked the respondent something about the doctrine of the substitutionary atonement. About half of these responses mention it—most affirming either their ignorance of Foster's views or his complicity with the doctrine.[24] Interestingly, when Foster graduated from seminary he delivered a graduation address entitled "Conservative Innovation," but reliable and complete sources for the contents of this speech are not available.[25] At the very least, the title seems to corroborate the evidence that Foster's general theological trajectory tended toward modernism.

As to the question of conservative or liberal, another former classmate at Rochester and PhD from Yale wrote a somewhat more nuanced answer. He saw Foster as believing himself to be conserving the essence and reconstructing only when necessary (this was alluded to above). In describing Foster's relationship to A. H. Strong's theology, this source thought

---

22. W. C. Taylor to Hjalmar Wilhelm Johnson, August 11, 1930, quoted in Johnson, "The Religious Thought of George B. Foster," 232n2. Several other classmates corroborate the congruence between Foster's views and Strong's on the same page.

23. D. T. Denman to Hjalmar Wilhelm Johnson, August 29, 1930, quoted in Johnson, "The Religious Thought of George B. Foster," 233n1. The overly positive bias of this quote, in view of Foster's later beliefs, indicates that it might be a bit of hagiography from a modernist admirer. This is confirmed later by Denman's support of Foster during Foster's conflict with the proto-fundamentalists.

24. Johnson, "The Religious Thought of George B. Foster," 227–39.

25. Johnson, "The Religious Thought of George B. Foster," 234.

it important to remark that Strong considered himself to be liberal, and some important Baptist institutions such as McMaster University thought Strong to be too liberal. The source goes on to say that Strong probably thought highly of Foster and recommended him first to McMaster and later to Chicago. It is also important to note that this information was retained in confidence, and Johnson was unable to reveal the source.[26]

W. C. Taylor, who was mentioned earlier, quoted Dr. Strong as stating during their last lecture in which he and Foster were present: "my young brethren, if you come to be thinkers, you will have your doubts, but do not bring your doubts before the people. Keep them to yourselves, live near the Savior and bye and bye the most or all of them will disappear." Johnson states that this remark was often quoted by Foster while teaching at University of Chicago.[27]

The nomenclature used to describe Foster's beliefs varies according to its source. The more liberal or modernist critic of Foster tended to equivocate on terms.[28] Their definitions of "liberal" or "modernist" are often compromised by their desire to put those ideas in their best light. Those who were of the theological profession and were more conservative, such as Purinton, tended to think Foster to have gone liberal at some point, but they do not equivocate on the terms.[29] Of those who were not seasoned theologians but family members and presumably orthodox, Mrs. Olive Foster

---

26. Anonymous to Hjalmar Wilhelm Johnson, September 5, 1930, quoted in Johnson, "The Religious Thought of George B. Foster," 236n1.

27. W. C. Taylor to Hjalmar Wilhelm Johnson, August 11, 1930, quoted in Johnson, "The Religious Thought of George B. Foster," 239n2.

28. I am well aware of the difficulty with these terms, but some readers may not be. Historically and theologically, nearly all theologians, biblical scholars, and churchmen of the Chicago School (Foster, Shailer Mathews, William Rainey Harper et al.) were modernists, complying with Cauthen's definition of "modernistic liberal." Men such as William Newton Clarke, Harry Emerson Fosdick, and Walter Rauschenbusch were "evangelical liberals." The modernists were generally more progressive than the liberals. For further explanation see Kenneth Cauthen, *The Impact of American Religious Liberalism* (New York: Harper & Row, 1962) 26–37. For the purpose of this article, the two terms are nearly synonymous. Primary sources very often do not recognize this distinction and being exacting about the taxonomy only confuses the narrative. It will suffice the reader to recognize that there are degrees and varieties of religious liberalism and modernism. It is my opinion that, in his full maturity, Foster stood as a transitional figure between Cauthen's ethical-social modernism and his empirical modernism.

29. Johnson notes that Purinton places the change of Foster's views at a time after he arrived back from Germany (Johnson, "The Religious Thought of George B. Foster," 246).

Hoover is an example. She notes that Foster's "gradual loss of faith—to be sure, this began before he went to Germany." [30]

University Professor

Upon graduation in 1887, Foster became pastor at Saratoga Springs, New York.[31] Just a few years later in 1891, Foster accepted the offer to teach at McMaster University, requiring a year of study abroad. He hesitated because he already had four children. A fifth child was actually born upon return from studying in Germany.[32] For a year's time, 1891–92, he studied in Germany at the Universities of Göttingen and Berlin.[33]

In June of 1892 Foster received the degree Doctor of Philosophy from Denison University of Granville, Ohio.[34] He began teaching at McMaster in the fall of 1892.[35] Some students noted that Foster's popularity was due to his open-mindedness in his quest for the truth.[36] The opinion of whether or not Foster was conservative or liberal was mixed among his former students at McMaster. He was never accused of denying orthodox doctrine or miracles, but there is a hint that he began to question the worth of the virgin birth and substitutionary atonement. In other words, he believed that the value for us in Christ does not rely upon these doctrines.[37] This hinted at the Ritschlianism to which he was exposed in Germany.

In 1895, Foster was recruited to become associate professor of Systematic Theology in the Divinity School of the newly formed University of Chicago. At Chicago he transformed into a charismatic figure capable of leading many students toward a new vision of Christianity. This new vision dared to accept the way modern criticism had decimated the old orthodoxy and sought to rebuild Christianity anew. Perhaps the phoenix as the emblem of

---

30. Olive Foster Hoover to Hjalmar Wilhelm Johnson, October 6, 1930, quoted in Johnson, "The Religious Thought of George B. Foster," 241 n. 1.
31. Johnson, "The Religious Thought of George B. Foster," 240.
32. Johnson, "The Religious Thought of George B. Foster," 242–44.
33. Johnson, "The Religious Thought of George B. Foster," 244.
34. Johnson, "The Religious Thought of George B. Foster," 247. The PhD was still a young degree and Foster submitted no dissertation. His education in Germany was credited toward the degree.
35. Johnson, "The Religious Thought of George B. Foster," 247.
36. Johnson, "The Religious Thought of George B. Foster," 251–52.
37. Johnson, "The Religious Thought of George B. Foster," 252–58.

the second University of Chicago symbolized more to Foster and the Divinity School than just the resurrection of the first failed University of Chicago. It may have alluded to Harper's dream for a modern resurrection of the Christian religion after its demise at the hands of the skeptic.

While at the University of Chicago, Foster began his writing career. Foster's writing was slim, and nearly half of his entire monographic corpus was published posthumously. Sometimes it evidenced such heavy editing that it might not be called his work anymore than the Tübingen School called the epistles outside the *Hauptbriefe* the work of Paul. The University of Chicago Press published Foster's *The Finality of the Christian Religion* in 1906 as part of its decennial publications. This volume helped brand Foster as Ebionite or Unitarian and subsequently managed to provide grounds for his expulsion from the Baptist Minister's Conference. This work greatly impressed Arnold who identified Foster as the "primal force" within the Chicago School. For Arnold, Foster's first book was to the Chicago School what Lombard's *Sentences* was to the medieval scholastics. It would set the very ethos of the institution. The subsequent theologians of the Chicago School would produce its *Summa Theologiae*.[38] Foster's second book would be *The Function of Religion in Man's Struggle for Existence* (1909). Unlike its predecessor, this volume proved to be shorter and a bit more accessible than his first volume.[39] After his death, one of Foster's students, D. C. Macintosh, would edit and publish *Christianity in Its Modern Expression*. The reliability of its representation of Foster's thought is doubtful because much of the content was merely a redaction of a portion of Foster's class notes. Macintosh worked with an edited compendium of Foster's classroom lecture notes, some from students. His second posthumously published work was edited by the secularist Curtis W. Reese and former colleague A. Eustace Hayden. This volume was a commentary on the thought and philosophy of Friedrich Nietzsche and seems to be more reliably representative of Foster's thought because there was an actual extant manuscript directly attributable to Foster.[40] These four books are the extent of Foster's entire monographic corpus. A quick search through

---

38. Arnold, *Near the Edge of Battle*, 28–29.

39. It was actually an address to the Philosophic Union of the State University of California in August 29, 1908. Later it was dictated and put into print. (George Burman Foster, *The Function of Religion in Man's Struggle for Existence* [Chicago: The University of Chicago Press, 1909] vii).

40. David Henry Koss, "The Development of Naturalism at the Divinity School of the University of Chicago with Special Emphasis on the Doctrine of God," PhD diss., Northwestern University, 1972, 19–21.

the indices of the journals in the field of religion and theology reveals that Foster frequently contributed articles and was published. He also contributed a number of book reviews, and these sometimes yield valuable information regarding the status of his theology.

Foster's career and theological life were not born out a comfortable or easy existence. Foster seemed to be a child of adversity and struggle. His students described him as being gentle and unflappable. Foster struck an unlikely friendship with the skeptical Clarence Darrow. The two held a number of debates, the transcripts of which are available still today.[41] In his debates with Clarence Darrow, he was ever the optimist and at Darrow's own admission would never stoop to pettiness or harshness in a debate:

> No man could quarrel with him as to his convictions. He was so tender and kindly, even to those with whom he disagreed, that often he left you with a belief that he felt and thought as you felt and thought. He was the fairest man in his attitude of mind that I ever knew. I seldom met him in debate that I did not afterwards apologize for something that I had said wherein I thought the lawyer had overcome the man. But, I can never remember the time where I thought any apology was due from him for any statement that was not absolutely fair and just.[42]

This sort of demeanor also seemed present at the times during which Foster underwent extreme sorrow and endured significant bereavement. Shailer Mathews recounted the first time that he met Foster. It was just subsequent to the drowning of one of Foster's children. With this ordeal as illustration, Mathews eulogized Foster as "one of the noblest and bravest souls I ever knew. He faced misfortunes with courage which was sublime."[43] Three sons and two daughters preceded George Burman Foster to the grave. One daughter died shortly before her wedding; and his

---

41. Two such examples are George Burman Foster and Clarence Darrow, *Do Humans Have Free Will? A Debate: Affirmative: Prof. George Burman Foster, Negative: Clarence Darrow* (Girard, KS: Haldeman-Julius, 1928); and George Burman Foster and Clarence Darrow, *Is Life Worth Living? Debate: Affirmative: Prof. George Burman Foster, Negative: Clarence Darrow* (Chicago: John F. Higgins Printer and Binder, 1917).

42. Clarence Darrow, *Remarks of Clarence Darrow at Memorial Services to George Burman Foster and at the Funeral of Jack P. Altgeld*, pamphlet (John F. Higgins, Printer, 1919) 5.

43. Shailer Mathews, *New Faith for Old: An Autobiography* (New York: Macmillan Company, 1936) 69.

son, Harrison, died of pneumonia in an army training camp.[44] Three of the others died at the hands of "the Great Destroyer."[45] His wife suffered from a nervous disorder.[46] William Fenn bemoans the fact that when Harrison died Foster related to him that the only clergyman in the city of Chicago to extend condolences was a Jewish rabbi.[47] Estrangement apparently magnified his bereavement.

Foster's sorrows were not limited to bereavement and estrangement, but his career met setbacks as well. After an address to an Iowa Baptist meeting, wherein Foster declared his modernist views in the most offensive yet forthright manner, his champion and president of the University, William Rainey Harper, could not allow the bad publicity to continue. This event combined with the same address offered at a Chicago Baptist Minister's Meeting and the increased involvement of the denomination in the affairs of the Divinity School led to Foster's transfer to the University. In 1905, William Rainey Harper, himself dying of cancer, moved Foster from the Divinity School to the University Graduate School as Professor of the Philosophy of Religion with the approval of the Advisory Committee. This occurrence, by all indications, seemed fortuitous to even Foster. His theological views had moved to such a degree that keeping his salary in a school that ostensibly sought to train ministers of the gospel might be considered inappropriate. The religious folk of the Midwest perceived Foster as proffering more doubt than faith. His honesty concerning the agenda of religious modernism worried those who believed such a direct approach to the issues would cause a reaction culminating in a loss of power. This did not fit Harper's ideal. Shailer Mathews, already a full professor in the Department of Systematic Theology, was called upon to fill the vacancy left by Foster. Mathews concealed the modernist agenda much better and was less open about any doubts he may have entertained.[48] Of the events

---

44. Alan Gragg, *George Burman Foster: Religious Humanist*, Perspectives in Religious Studies (Danville, VA: Association of Baptist Professors of Religion, 1978) 2.

45. J. M. Powis Smith in University of Chicago, "Foster Memorial Service," 174.

46. Gragg, *George Burman Foster*, 2.

47. William Wallace Fenn in University of Chicago, "Foster Memorial Service," 179.

48. Mathews was decidedly more politically adept than Foster and frequently displayed the nuancing style of a politician. So much so that a remark was made in the 1920s about Mathews: "What is Modernism?"

"That is what Shailer Mathews teaches at the University of Chicago."

"What is fundamentalism?"

"That is what Shailer Mathews preaches to the Northern Baptist Convention." (Shailer

precipitating Foster's move from the Divinity School to the University, some attribute Harper's decision to Foster's interaction with the Baptist Advisory Committee. Apparently, because of Foster's views, the committee was inclined to separate the Divinity School from the University; a measure Harper did not want to take. The openly radical views expressed by Foster did little to help his position in the seminary. He was labeled an atheist or a Unitarian.[49] Harper's disappointment concerning Foster is evident in his letter to Mr. and Mrs. John B. Stetson, the benefactor and benefactress of Stetson University in Deland, Florida:

> Dr. Foster is one of the best men I have ever known, but keeps putting his foot into trouble as rapidly as any man I have ever known. We have stood by him bravely, but he seems to have no thought that people must be educated before they can enjoy or appreciate or even approve of his position. His address at the opening of the Divinity School last autumn was exceedingly unfortunate. Quite recently he has been carrying on correspondence with some Baptist ministers who belong to the narrowest set. He has overlooked the fact that he was writing to men who could not understand him, and consequently has given them a basis for attack, which will be quite serious.[50]

In *The Finality of the Christian Religion*, Foster sought to support the view that, while other religions may have truth about God in them, Christianity was the best and most complete. This was a current and popular view of the era. The irony was that Foster destroyed this popular view in this work. His accomplishment caused no small problem for himself and the University.[51] Foster's transfer from the Divinity School to the

---

Mathews, "The Life and Thought of Shailer Mathews," introduction, Kenneth Cauthen in *Jesus on Social Institutions* [Philadelphia: Fortress, 1971] xxii). Hynes makes the observation that Mathews was more practical than philosophical. Foster was philosophical and thus undermined with his teaching evangelical zeal. This infuriated the Midwestern orthodoxy and prompted his transfer to the University Graduate School. Foster's disciple, A. Eustace Haydon, continued many of his mentor's pursuits but from within the Humanities Department as Professor of Comparative Religions (Hynes, *Shirley Jackson Case*, 120.).

49. W Creighton Peden, "The Chicago School (1906–1926) in American Religious Thought," *Ultimate Reality and Meaning* 6, no. 1 (1983) 26.

50. William Rainey Harper to Mr. and Mrs. John B. Stetson, February 29, 1904. Harper, William Rainey. Presidents Papers, 1889–1925, [Box 34, Folder 2], Special Collections Research Center, Joseph M. Regenstein Library, University of Chicago.

51. Peden, "The Chicago School (1906–1926) in American Religious Thought," 27.

University Graduate School did not affect his influence upon the Divinity students. Harper had envisioned a university in which all the departments existed somewhat symbiotically. The Divinity school students were given the freedom to take courses from other departments within the university and apply the credits toward their degree. The vast majority of Foster's students, while he was teaching in the Graduate School, were from the Divinity School.[52] After labeling Foster an "academic adolescent," Koss goes on to attribute this to the Chicago School: "Foster was the first of the school to publish a major radical work, the first to be hunted for heresy, and the first of the major theological teachers to die (leaving much unwritten than [sic] he planned to publish)."[53]

Foster continued to teach in the Graduate School until his death on December 22, 1918. Toward the end of his life he had pastored a Unitarian church in Madison, Wisconsin, traveling from Chicago to Madison every week. He had been good friends with President Van Hise of the University of Wisconsin, and when President Van Hise died, Foster conducted the funeral in foul weather. From this he seemed to have been sufficiently weakened so as to contract a cold that would eventually lead to his death. The exact cause of his death was an infection of the spleen.[54]

The Proto-Fundamentalist Fight with Foster

The summer of 1909 proved to be a typically warm Chicago summer, but George Burman Foster felt its heat in more ways than one. Denominational newspapers and city newspapers across North America carried the news of

---

52. Koss asserts that Foster himself planned his departure from the Divinity School under the arrangement mentioned above. This allowed him to operate without the visibility that would garner the criticism of conservatives. (Koss, "The Development of Naturalism at the Divinity School of the University of Chicago," 15). Interesting artifacts were found in the course of my research in between the leaves of one of Foster's notebooks: several class attendance tickets from the spring quarter of 1916 and summer quarter of 1918 from a Comparative Religion course. Apparently the notes were used to teach that course. Three of five students indicated that they were part of the Divinity School (George Burman Foster. "Primitive Religion," vol. 2. Papers [Box 1, Folder 2], Special Collections Research Center, Joseph M. Regenstein Library, University of Chicago, n.d., n.p.).

53. Koss, "The Development of Naturalism at the Divinity School of the University of Chicago," 51–52.

54. J. V. Nash, "A Twentieth Century Emancipator," The Open Court 36, no. 6 (June 1922) 328.

Foster's controversy with the more conservative Baptist clergyman in emotionally charged editorials and tabloid-like reports. Articles about Foster's problems found a place on the front page of the *Chicago Daily Tribune*. The conservatives of the Northern Baptists in Chicago demanded that their money no longer support infidels. Foster was the first to fall victim to the Baptist equivalent of a heresy trial.

Foster's conflicts with conservatives, however, started well before 1909. Rumors abounded of things amiss at McMaster during the twilight years of the 19th century, traceable to Foster. Once at Chicago, Foster candidly expressed his unorthodox views in ministers' meetings, University addresses, and personal correspondence with enough regularity that it caused President Harper much consternation, testing even Harper's resolve in matters of academic freedom. In 1905 as mentioned above, Harper managed to have Foster moved from the Divinity School to the University. Foster's first book, *The Finality of the Christian Religion*, must have been at least a preliminary draft stage by this point. The publication of the University of Chicago's first theological monograph in 1906 gave rise to the start of the next incoming salvo directed at the University from conservative Northern Baptist ministers. This debate began in February of 1906, less than a month after the death of Harper. The acting president, T. W. Goodspeed, and the incoming president, Harry Pratt Judson (1849–1927), would both be tested by the conservatives' reactions to Foster's *Finality*. The debate, commenced in February 1906 would run through April of the same year. Then it seemingly disappeared from the pages of denominational and city newspapers. It resurfaced in June 1909 after Foster published his second book and conservatives became aware of some of the more heretical material he had been writing for the journals.

The controversy between Foster and the conservatives began in earnest after the publication of Foster's *Finality* in 1906. President Harper made his decision to remove Foster from the Divinity School in a calculated manner. He preserved the University and his principles of academic freedom by partially disarming the conservatives before the argument turned brutal. The decision was made on February 15, 1905, and Foster took up the new position officially on April 1, 1905. From that former date to the latter, the controversy between Foster and the conservatives escalated as reported in both the *Chicago Daily Tribune* and *The Standard*. The reports of the *Tribune* highlighted the controversy, while *The Standard* called for even-handed debate, allowing both sides to have their say. At least six reports, in tabloid fashion, managed to be printed in the *Tribune* before *The Standard* published a plea for more irenic discourse. Speaking of Foster's *Finality*, the editors of *The Standard* argued that "it ought not to be denounced—or praised—until it has been thoroughly considered."[55] Conservatives John Roach Straton, Austen K. De Blois, and Johnston Myers all denounced Foster in letters to the editor of *The Standard*.

On March 10, 1906, proto-fundamentalists of the Chicago Baptist Minister's Meeting put this motion on the floor:

> Whereas, a member of this conference has issued from the University of Chicago Press a book entitled "The Finality of the Christian Religion."
>
> Resolved, that we as a conference declare it to be our resolute conviction that the views set forth in this book are contrary to scripture, and that its teaching and tendency are subversive of the vital and essential truths of the Christian faith.[56]

The same issue of *The Standard* reports on the protest of the minority at the Ministers' Meeting. The minority asserted that the resolution "misrepresent[ed] the position and violat[ed] the rights of the minority."[57] The minority disagreed with the majority because they alleged that the majority "assumed functions belonging only to a delegated council."[58] Further, the protesting minority accused the majority of "tending either to throttle free speech or to convert the conference into an inquisitorial body."[59] The signatories included Shailer Mathews, T. W. Goodspeed, Earnest D. Burton, Daniel T. Denman (who has been mentioned above), and others.[60] This protest was countered in the subsequent issue of *The Standard* by Austen K. de Blois, wherein De Blois would declare "If I agreed with the teachings of [Foster's *Finality*], I would leave the Christian ministry, and at once."[61]

By the end of April 1906 the controversy quietly slipped from the pages of *The Standard*. Apparently, the *Chicago Daily Tribune* editors grew

---

55. J. S. Dickerson and R. N. Van Doren, "The Foster Incident," *The Standard*, February 24, 1906, 4.
56. "Chicago and Vicinity," *The Standard*, March 10, 1906, 17.
57. "A Protest," *The Standard*, March 10, 1906, 18.
58. "A Protest," 18.
59. "A Protest," 18.
60. "A Protest," 18.
61. Austen K. de Blois, "A Protest and a Protest," *The Standard*, March 17, 1906, 13.

weary much earlier and had little, if anything, to say about this issue after February 10, 1906.

In 1909, the matter of Foster's problems resurfaced largely on account of the fact that he had promised a second volume and his supporters had urged forbearance until this more constructive volume appeared.[62] That year he published *The Function of Religion in Man's Struggle for Existence*. It did little to assure conservatives of Foster's orthodoxy.

With Foster clearly demonstrating unorthodox beliefs, continuing to demonstrate a habit of iconoclastic speech, and preaching at the Third Unitarian church in Chicago, orthodox Baptists were to receive a "new jolt."[63] Dr. Johnston Myers of Immanuel Baptist church led the charge to have Foster's ordination revoked, his membership in the Chicago Baptist Ministers' Conference dropped, and his tenure removed from the faculty of the University of Chicago. No less than twenty-three articles were reported in the *Chicago Daily Tribune* regarding Foster's doctrinal infidelity. Even *The Standard* began to distance itself from Foster, while at the same time it maintained that his dismissal from the Conference would not solve the problem.[64]

Eventually, Myers, although replaced as the charge's leader by A. C. Dixon (1854–1925),[65] would have his way. On June 22, 1909, the *Chicago Daily Tribune* reported that the Chicago Baptist Ministers' Conference had ejected him from its membership. The paper contended that this action "practically barred" Foster "from preaching in any Baptist pulpit in the country."[66] Indeed, the press found Foster's expulsion from the conference to be such good copy that the *Tribune* gleefully printed a nice size photograph of Foster with the headline, "Barred from Pulpits as a Heretic."[67]

After Foster's expulsion from the Conference, some of the conservatives began to make moves to investigate the University of Chicago. Rather diplomatically, Rev. John A. Earl of Beldon Avenue Baptist Church[68] sug-

---

62. "Defies Critics of Foster," *Chicago Daily Tribune*, February 13, 1906, 14.

63. "Orthodoxy Gets New Jolt," *Chicago Daily Tribune*, March 29, 1909, 1.

64. J. S. Dickerson and R. N. Van Doren, "The Case of Professor Foster," *The Standard*, June 19, 1909, 4.

65. For a brief narrative on Dixon's involvement in the Foster affair see Gerald L. Priest, "A. C. Dixon, Chicago Liberals, and *The Fundamentals*," *Detroit Baptist Seminary Journal*, 1 (Spring 1996) 113–34.

66. "Baptist Pulpits Shut to Foster," *Chicago Daily Tribune*, June 22, 1909, 1.

67. "Barred from Pulpits as a Heretic," *Chicago Daily Tribune*, June 22, 1909, 2.

68. This is an interesting connection in view of the fact that in 1932 the separatist

gested that such an investigation would be useless. Consequently, Myers withdrew his resolution to perform the investigation.⁶⁹ Foster's theology never again surfaced as a fight in the Convention. He was spared from losing his faculty position and he retained his ordination credentials. Foster's troubles quietly faded away, probably more due to the exhaustion of his critics than their resolution with his doctrine.

Gragg argues that the Foster debacle began to solidify the positions of conservative or orthodox and liberal or modernist. He notes that among fruits of *The Finality of the Christian Religion* was the cleavage of the Illinois Baptist State Association from the Northern Baptists to join the Southern Baptist Convention and the founding of Northern Baptist Theological Seminary in 1913 to offset the liberal influence of the Divinity School of the University of Chicago.⁷⁰ If this is the case, then Foster's questionable doctrine served the purpose of sounding the alarm by causing orthodox Baptists to become a self-conscious religious movement that would give rise to the later fundamentalists within the next two decades.

Theology

Theological Formation

As has been noted earlier, the exact timing of Foster's change from his orthodox roots to his modernist maturity bears a great uncertainty. Arguably, the time matters little. Two observations may be made regarding Foster's theological development. First, he greatly admired A. H. Strong, and followed in his sort of orthodox progressivism. Second, we may note the general trajectory of Foster's thought. He tended toward the desire for an unfettered intellect able to judge anything and everything within its perceptive grasp. In fact, in his later maturity, Foster's marked repudiation of what he called "authority-religion" matches this spirit. Gragg remarks that he sees the evidence of modernism in Foster's review of Robert L. Ottley's (1856–1933) work on the incarnation published in 1896. He maintains that

---

Baptist group the General Association of Regular Baptist Churches would experience its genesis here. Robert T. Ketcham would be pastor at this church.

69. "Rift in Baptist Conference," *Chicago Daily Tribune*, June 29, 1909, 6.

70. Alan Gragg, "George Burman Foster (1858–1918)," in *Dictionary of Heresy Trials in American Christianity*, ed. George H. Shriver (Westport, CT: Greenwood, 1997) 147.

Foster made remarks indicating that he had left orthodoxy, but Foster's critique seems too oblique to substantiate this.[71]

Johnson begins his work on Foster with an overview of the philosophic and theological landscape prior to Foster. He begins with Descartes and ends with Kaftan just before giving commentary on the subject of his dissertation. Of the most closely related philosophers and theologians to Foster in time, Johnson notes the influence of Ritschl, Kaftan, Troeltsch and Lotze.[72] Hynes sees Foster as being heavily influenced by the Neo-Kantians, more so than other members of the Chicago School.[73] Koss sees the same intellectual heritage and rather illustriously describes its effects on Foster:

> To the grieving George Burman Foster an intellectual (i.e., existential for this intellect) battle of Armageddon was waging, with the debunkers and underminers of the traditional Christian faith certain of victory. Of the defenders of the faith, only the moderate liberals of the Christocentric school had offered any intellectually respectable hope, but to Foster they must have seemed like Ethelred the Unready paying off a Canute who could collect tribute and be king of England in the end anyway. To continue the image, Foster was like a tenth century Englishman, born and bred a loyal subject of King Ethelred, whose royal folly and blundering he could only too pitifully see, but an Englishman who realistically knew Canute's power, actually admired the Dane's supremacy and foresaw without benefit of prophecy the inevitable result.[74]

Foster, at some point in his life, broached this dilemma wherein, believing he was saving his faith, he gave away the very sentiments that granted it to him. This path bore a painful familiarity with many of both the liberals and the modernists. Thinking they were preserving the faith from the onslaughts of scientific inquiry, they capitulated on the very matters

---

71. Gragg, "Formative Influences on George Burman Foster," 3. Although an examination of Foster's review of Ottley's work (George Burman Foster, review of *The Doctrine of the Incarnation*, *The Biblical World* 8, no. 6 [December 1896] 508–10) reveals that Foster only seems to be criticizing Ottley for not bringing the discussion of the incarnation into the contemporary scholarly debate, not necessarily for holding to an orthodox position.

72. Johnson, "The Religious Thought of George B. Foster," 265.

73. Hynes, *Shirley Jackson Case*, 95.

74. Koss, "The Development of Naturalism at the Divinity School of the University of Chicago," 12.

of faith most vulnerable to scientific inquiry and, at the same time, most necessary for a meaningful faith.

Foster obviously develops modernistic beliefs sometime between his seminary days and Germany. After studying in Germany, as we shall see later, he tends toward the moderating position of Ritschlianism. By 1906, it becomes evident from his first major publication that he has moved to his own significantly more radical position that is at once humanistic, pragmatic, and mystical. By 1909, Foster demonstrates that he is beyond modernism and well beyond liberal religionism.

Higher Criticism

Foster accepted the claims of higher criticism as most theologians in his position did. Given William Rainey Harper's (1856–1906) dream of a university that makes use of all the modern ways of discovering knowledge in all fields, it is highly unlikely that, at the time of his hiring, Harper would even consider Foster if he firmly rejected the critical research of the era. The theologically mature Foster repeatedly made remarks concerning the role of higher criticism in the demise of his own ideological bogeyman, authority-religion:

> In authority-religion the Bible is an effect to be referred to miraculous divine causalities. The eighteenth-century criticism of deist, rationalist, and mystic, and the historical-critical movement of the nineteenth century, are decisive against this foundation of the value of the Bible. The Bible was not "automatically composed," is due rather to the "free caprice of the writers," and exhibits scientific and historic errors, expresses local and personal passions—in a word, has all the marks of a deliberate human composition.[75]

The entire text of the first part of Foster's *Finality* is nothing but a critique of Christianity's epistemological centers for authority. Foster, following what he believed to be the evolution of the church, recounted the destruction of both ecclesiastical authority and tradition. Then, as if embarking on another Reformation, he assumed the destructive critical measures taken up against Scripture and deemed them as reliable. His discussion of miracles was enough to make even fellow modernists uncomfortable. In his usual straightforward style, Foster assailed the belief

---

75. George Burman Foster, *The Finality of the Christian Religion* (Chicago: The University of Chicago Press, 1906) 112.

in miracles. He brought to bear the reasoning of Spinoza, Hume, and Kant. In his fervor, he turned on his former professor A. H. Strong, who had explained the miracle at Cana to coincide with the principle of analogy by noting that even as God turns the moisture of the earth into the wine of grapes today, even so did he at the wedding feast in Cana.[76] To this Foster caustically replies:

> [T]he tacit syllogism of the distinguished dogmatician and ecclesiastic is as follows: The kind of occurrence which certainly happens today could have happened in the past, since nature is uniform; miracles, witness what goes on in grapevines and cornstalks, occur today; therefore miracles occurred in the past; witness the turning of water into wine at Cana! And yet we wonder that the intelligent public has lost confidence in its religious leaders.[77]

Consequently, Foster saw religion as merely the product of human imagination. Foster's turn to a humanistic explanation for religion rather than revelation arose because of a change in the accepted cosmology making the supernatural witnessed to within the revelation untenable. His solution was to provide a god described as a great immanent causality.[78]

Ritschlianism[79]

The exact connection of Foster to the teachings of Ritschl appears to be almost anecdotal. He had been in Germany and studying in the same schools as the leading disciples of Ritschl, but it is difficult to ascertain the exact influence on Foster by the Ritschlian School. If there was any marked influence, it would be transitory and partial in nature. Even if

---

76. Foster, *The Finality of the Christian Religion*, 128.
77. Foster, *The Finality of the Christian Religion*, 129.
78. Gragg, "Formative Influences on George Burman Foster," 10.
79. Ritchlianism is a school of liberal Protestant theology founded by Albrecht Ritschl (1822–89). While agreeing in substance to the attitude toward revelation and miracles as Kant, Schleiermacher, and the religious liberals of his day; Ritschl added at least three unique contributions to liberal theology that seemed, at the time, to make it a sort of compromise between liberal and conservative doctrine. First, he retained the importance of a real Jesus who is god-like God and who was the founder of the church. Second, he believed that faith which justifies is possible only within the church. Third, he believed that Christianity was important because it provided a basis upon which to make value judgments.

Foster did not accept the Ritschlian schema completely, he seemed to adopt certain Ritschlian concepts.

It seems more plausible to conclude that Foster emphasized some aspects of Ritschlian thinking at the expense of others. Foster's principle of freedom excluded the necessity of any authority whether that be church, state, or Bible in view of a believing person.[80] He preferred freedom even before virtue. Gragg asserts that Foster was influenced deeply by Ritschlianism as it was the most potent force operating in the realm of religion in that era. He took from it its rejection of orthodoxy and its emphasis on personal freedom and autonomy—even the concept of a personal redeemer:[81]

> What is the problem of the present hour which paralyzes some with dread and exhilarates others with enthusiasm? The emancipation of religion from religion, morality from morality, theology from theology. The theological task today in all western Christendom is the completion of Luther's Reformation, the disengagement of our Protestantism from the remainders of Roman Catholicism, the complete rejection of the false principle of authority.[82]

Parts of Foster's *Christianity in Its Modern Expression*, prepared before 1905, seem to give evidence of the standard Ritschlian model of theology. The footnotes are some of the later and more extemporaneous remarks that he made in class. These give evidence that Foster was moving leftward from Ritschl and his school.[83] Even in his *Finality*, the more mature estimation of his life's work, Foster's expressions echo Ritschlian ideas with respect to what he viewed to be the god-like human, but only human, Jesus in the founding of the church: "Even this we can understand, viz., that precisely this mystery of a creative revelation-person has become the greatest agency for founding community, that faith in Jesus founded the church."[84]

Hynes' connection of Foster to Ritschlianism is less pronounced. He does not mention Foster being directly influenced by the Ritschlian School. He makes a general comment about the fact that many in the Chicago School did come under its influence, especially citing Case and Mathews.[85]

---

80. Gragg, "Formative Influences on George Burman Foster," 3.

81. Gragg, "Formative Influences on George Burman Foster," 4.

82. George B. Foster, "The Theological Training for the Times," *The Biblical World* 9, no. 1 (January 1897) 24.

83. Gragg, "Formative Influences on George Burman Foster," 11.

84. Foster, *The Finality of the Christian Religion*, 393.

85. In fact, Hynes lists this as a possible future research project: "A detailed study

Pragmatism

Foster's Ritschlian tendencies in Christology gradually gave way to his own radical tendencies. Foster never denied that Jesus was the manifestation of God; he merely would not say that Jesus was God:

> And Jesus was what he taught, and taught what he was. But it must be that God is as good as Jesus is. Then we may have the faith which the gospel requires—faith in God the Father, in his fatherly grace in forgiving sins, and in an eternal life.[86]

Foster moves, during his teaching career from being Christian, in the sense of seeing a necessity in Christ for a valid and final religion, to denying the uniqueness and necessity of Christ. His transfer to the University from the Divinity School seems to correspond with this movement.[87] The authority of Scripture, for Foster, became subject to the pragmatic need of the hour:

> Beneath the surface there is something that might without much extravagance be called epoch-making in all this, viz., the appreciation of the Bible, not from the mode of its origin, but from the end that it serves—"not by its roots, but its fruits." The criterion of miraculous supernaturalism according to authority-religion yields to the criterion of serviceability.[88]

Much of the logic in Foster's pragmatism is captured in prose that is difficult to penetrate, and most of the historical material is based upon reports of extemporaneously delivered material.[89]

History of Religion and *The Finality of the Christian Religion*

Foster built the majority of his reconstruction of the Christian faith on the system that had served Harnack so well. He saw the evolution of

---

of each Chicago figure's relationship to Ritschlianism might prove a most interesting project" (Hynes, *Shirley Jackson Case*, 96).

86. Foster, *The Finality of the Christian Religion*, 518.
87. Gragg, "Formative Influences on George Burman Foster," 20.
88. Foster, *The Finality of the Christian Religion*, 92.
89. Gragg, *George Burman Foster*, 13–14. This work of Gragg's, in addition to his dissertation, provides a great deal of information from reports that are not easily accessible.

doctrine as the best argument against holding fast to any static articulation by an authority of any sort—against any a deposit of revelation, whether it be a church or some ensconced holy writ. He clearly saw his contemporary modern era as another pivotal time in the development of doctrine. Following a discussion of how the refutation of Aristotle by means of modern inventions caused people, fearing change, to spurn the instruments of observation, he says:

> With the means of investigation afforded by these inventions the new science possessed an inexhaustible fountain from which it could draw independent strength, cast off the yoke of every authority, and receive from the hands of nature that gift of God after which the modern man had begun to yearn and to struggle—namely, *the freedom of the human spirit*.[90]

He did not even revere the Reformers, Luther and Melanchthon, but saw their criticism of new scientific discovery as a sort of faithlessness: "They were indignant, grieved, and panicky, because the new view subverted the old, and because they had assumed as a matter of course that the old view concerning the universe was an inalienable constituent of the Christian religion."[91] He followed the argument, attempting to demonstrate that their own rejection of ecclesiastical authority only partially instituted reform. Further reformation was necessary in order to be more consistent in the total overthrow of authority. In Foster's view, the principle of *sola Scriptura* must be amended to allow for a not-so-static revelation. His main point was to make sure that his students understood that the modern understanding of the universe had changed the perception of revelation. This particular statement seems to conform to a more Hegelian panentheism that displaces Scripture with natural revelation:

> Thus religious ideas experienced and internalizing and spiritualizing, conformably to the new apprehension of the world. It follows that revelation, for example, is no longer to be thought of as a supernatural communication of divine instruction, guaranteed to be divine by the miraculous mode of its origin. Revelation is

---

90. George Burman Foster. "Dogma and Freedom," Papers, [Box 6, Folder 5], Special Collections Research Center, Joseph M. Regenstein Library, University of Chicago. The George Burman Foster papers span the span the years of 1897–1917. There is virtually no personal correspondence in these records. The collection consists of class lecture notes, manuscripts and typescripts for publication and lecture, and sermons. The original manuscript for *The Finality of the Christian Religion* is cataloged here.

91. Foster, "Dogma and Freedom," 7–8.

> an immanent divine self-expression and self-realization. It is historical and not apocalyptic, moral and magical, constant and not intermittent, universal not particular. For God is the God of the whole world and not of a fraction of it, of all religions, and not of one only. So, too, heaven is no longer a locality, but an ideal; not a cosmic region, but a cosmic value. The same is true of hell. The stories of the ascension of Jesus into heaven and descent into hell must be interpreted accordingly. They thereby cease to be records of historical and cosmological facts.[92]

Once he delivered revelation to whim of modernity, he turned to orthodoxy and its methodology for attaining truth and pronounced it dead:

> Precisely at the time when the folly of the omniscience and omnipotence of man was narrowing religion, comprehending heaven and earth by the dogmas of his wisdom, managing the whole world according to his own will by the magic formulas of his prayers and offerings, a pious genius gradually the omniscient and omnipotent man to which he did not and could not know and do,—to the lilies of the field and the birds of the air, as to whose bloom and whose life man was at the end of his wits, because this life welled up out of the infinite itself,—then on to man himself in whose soul were hidden abysses of life which no one could fathom, but which yet caught the echoes of a compassion, a righteousness and perfection, whose home and hearth are in the bosom of the infinite, in the heart of the heavenly father, and whose whisper to man declares that he is not what he has become, but what he is endowed to become, that he himself is an infinite becoming. The death of religion! What was killing religion was that old theology which would interrogate on the fathers of the church and the decisions of the councils, in order to solve all the riddles of the world, and which gave man an infallible, all-sufficient answer to the questions of his life so that he need have no doubts of his own and no dangers to escape.[93]

Foster's entire *Finality* was to prove the death of authority-religion and move on to a religion of freedom and spirit that retains only the God-idea and the example of Jesus: "Religion once free, it could freely unfold itself from within. The strength and purity of Jesus' faith in God were a result.

---

92. Foster, "Dogma and Freedom," 12–13.
93. Foster, "Dogma and Freedom," 15–16.

Once for All Delivered to the Saints

The form of his faith in God, the God-idea, may be changed, but the content will hardly be surpassed."[94]

Along with a view of the world that saw a transcendent God immanently working in creation, came a reformulation of the idea of Eternity. Eternity is immanent in time.[95] This reconstruction of Christianity appears consonant with his personal papers and notes:

> The history of Christian theology is the history of its dissolution and its disintegration. There was a time when theology was honored as queen of the sciences in the things . . . of the spirit—Divinity!—could there be anything loftier than a science, not of the ____, but of God—a revelation received from God himself; key to everything which might transpire in heaven or on earth, or under the Earth? Thus this theology deified everything that it touched with its magic wand: the work and sentences which it uttered; the deeds which were done according to its precepts; above all, the men who narrated to others the divine history, and who performed the divine miracles in the Church. There was only one thing that abjured its power and the was the earth, nature! But because man, the theologians _____, lives in nature, and could not be without nature, there was an inevitable conflict between the theological world and the natural world. Our theology has suffered one defeat after another in this conflict. As soon as theology was deprived of political power, the weapon with which it adduced tangible proof of its divinity it had to surrender the field to its opponent, step by step—to be sure, not without outwardly veiling its defeat behind the news of a brilliant victory. When natural science twisted miraculous omnipotence out of the hand of the priests, theology hid behind the _____ which the natural investigation recognized to his own knowledge - and shouted: Behold, precisely behind these _____ is the miracle is the supernatural revelation,—natural science itself as acknowledged our miracle, authenticated our revelation![96]

Koss believes that Foster followed the personalistic idealism of Borden Parker Bowne (1847–1910) insofar as he could affirm the personality

---

94. Foster, *The Finality of the Christian Religion*, 517.

95. Foster, *The Finality of the Christian Religion*, 171–74.

96. George Burman Foster, "The New God," Papers, [Box 6, Folder 1], Special Collections Research Center, Joseph M. Regenstein Library, University of Chicago. Handwritten MS, blanks indicate words in the source's handwriting that were not readable.

of God, but he would not view God as a person.[97] Foster affirmed this, noting that person seems too mundane and inadequate for God.[98]

Foster provided perhaps the most extensive treatment of miracles in his writing when compared with other religious modernists of his day. While he allowed for the possibility of Jesus' healing miracles, he would not allow for any miracle that openly flaunted the rules of nature.[99] Foster rejected the necessity of the resurrection of Christ. He averred that faith could not be placed in an historical event.[100]

Criticism of Science

Unlike the predominate swell of modernity, Foster deplored the mechanistic and deterministic ideas of modernity. From his Neo-Kantian perspective and perhaps from the wrong side of Lessing's ditch, Foster commented on the problem of calling dogmatics science because "[h]ow can the invisible spiritual reality affirmed by faith become an object of scientific investigation and exposition?"[101] He would not assign dogmatics to either science or historical theology but to the category "normative" as he says the *Encyclopaedia of Theology* does.[102]

Foster found himself in a situation that was familiar to all religious liberals:

> Liberals felt they were fighting on two fronts. On the right they were locked in battle with orthodoxy. On the left they were also obliged to wage battle with those who had gone too far in some of the very principles the liberal fought for. Every age has its *Schwaermer*, which a reforming Luther must attack in order to show that he is not guilty of theological extremism. This was especially true of all the "Chicago School" who could always find those to the left of themselves who had slipped into grave error. George Burman Foster attacked what he labeled as "naturalism"

97. Koss, "The Development of Naturalism at the Divinity School of the University of Chicago," 44–45.

98. George Burman Foster, Douglas Clyde Macintosh, ed., *Christianity in Its Modern Expression* (New York: Macmillan Company, 1921) 164.

99. Foster, *The Finality of the Christian Religion*, 22.

100. Peden, "The Chicago School (1906–1926) in American Religious Thought," 30.

101. George Burman Foster, "Christian Dogmatics," Papers, [Box 7, Folder 5], Special Collections Research Center, Joseph M. Regenstein Library, University of Chicago, 1.

102. Foster, "Christian Dogmatics," 3.

as the error to the left. It had to be combated because it was a new dogmatic; it was materialistic; it lacked appreciation for mystery; it was ignorant of the "plus" beyond nature; it was purposeless; and it lacked faith.[103]

Foster rejected both supernaturalism and naturalism. He regarded supernaturalism as unscientific and naturalism as lacking in mysteriousness.[104]

Religious Humanism

There is much difficulty in using Foster's work on Nietzsche in order to determine Foster's opinion of Nietzsche. Students of Foster's legacy disagree on the nature and extent of Foster's sympathies with Nietzsche. Koss contradicts Gragg when he remarks that the work on Nietzsche was merely expositional or explicatory but not apologetic. For Foster, Koss relates, there was no agreement with the concept of *Übermensch* (superman). The elitism of Nietzsche would be repugnant to Foster.[105] Foster's admiration of Nietzsche, however, cannot be so easily dismissed. As it was already demonstrated, Foster maintained that religion was a human invention. For Foster, it had no direct revelatory correlation to God. Religion was thought up to meet the needs of the situation. Foster concludes that Nietzsche concurs with him on this point. Of Foster's *Finality*, Reese says:

> The publication in 1906 of his *The Finality of the Christian Religion* created a storm, the echoes of which still reverberate in Christian circles. this work was followed in 1909 by *The Function of Religion in Man's Struggle for Existence*. Deep in understanding and broad in scholarship, George Burman Foster shook the very foundations of orthodoxy and contributed in a large way to the present humanistic trend in religion.[106]

Later, in his preface, Reese had this to say: "it was natural for Professor Foster, himself of Zarathustrian spirit, to become interested in Friedrich

---

103. Koss, "The Development of Naturalism at the Divinity School of the University of Chicago," 36.

104. Foster, *The Finality of the Christian Religion*, 207.

105. Koss, "The Development of Naturalism at the Divinity School of the University of Chicago," 21.

106. George Burman Foster, Curtis W. Reese, and A. Eustace Haydon, eds., *Friedrich Nietzsche* (New York: Macmillan Company, 1931) v–vi.

Nietzsche and to interpret him generously."[107] A careful reading of the text will confirm this estimation. To be sure, Foster did not follow in Nietzsche's atheism, but he was immensely sympathetic. He understood that the way in which Nietzsche's perspective had unfolded and left him in this dire position. The lack of a religion or atheism was just as valid of a response given Nietzsche's personal experience. In this, the biographer must wonder if Foster saw his friend, Clarence Darrow, in Nietzsche:

That Nietzsche felt deeply and painfully this loss of God—that there was nothing flippant, boastful, supercilious, or arrogant in connection with this experience, is evident from the fact that in all his works he speaks of the death of God as the most noteworthy event in the whole history of humanity, as the most formidable overthrowing in the history of human existence.[108]

Foster sees futility in finding some proof for God with a means that is ineffective because what is known has already been made known: "Few things in Nietzsche's writing have impressed me more than the discourse of a madman running about in the clear daylight, lantern in hand, looking for God."[109] This is also where he departs from Nietzsche. Nietzsche could not apprehend God by faith. Foster accepted the existence of God by faith even if the effects he had to look at seemed inadequate to the task. No church or revelation could provide anymore proof than what was in the world already. Nietzsche chose not to believe. Foster chose to believe on the sparest of evidence.

In some of Foster's ideas one can read a sort of Nietzschian "God is dead" thinking. For Foster, however, it was not that God was actually dead, it was that the orthodox concept of a transcendent God had outlived its usefulness as men progressed in their understanding and cultural evolution.[110]

Peden describes Foster's "God" as an ideal, not actual personality. This is in part supported by Foster's contention that the attributes that we give God must be present within ourselves (sort of a perverse twist on the Abelardian ontological argument). It is part of Foster's idea that religion and God ideas are manmade. Pragmatism is the ultimate judge

107. Foster et al., *Friedrich Nietzsche*, vi.
108. Foster et al., *Friedrich Nietzsche*, 221–22.
109. Foster et al., *Friedrich Nietzsche*, 222.
110. For a good article written near the advent of the "Death of God" theology on Foster's interaction with Nietzsche see C. Harvey Arnold, "The Dithyramb of Dionysus: The Impact of Friedrich Nietzsche on George Burman Foster, Professor Theology and Philosophy of Religion, 1885–1918," *Criterion* 7, no. 3 (Spring 1968) 29–40.

of religion's worth.¹¹¹ Consequently, Foster believed that we are not born persons, but that we become persons.¹¹² Peden also notes that after the death of his daughter in 1910, Foster's life came more under the influence of grief rather than scholarship. He notes, "Some argue that Foster tempered his humanistic religion during these years," but that there is insufficient scholarship to prove this.¹¹³

Conclusion

Foster's contribution to theology was more ground-breaking than substantial. He erected no superstructure on the ground he excavated. The paucity of complete works and his all too common tortured prose made Foster inaccessible for most. In Foster's ideas, the historian sees the territory that was taken by later theologians. Ames and Wieman would push beyond Foster's foundation toward a more complete humanism. It seems clear that Foster, while revering Christianity, was not wed to the necessity of its eternality. In this way, he foreshadowed the radical changes to come in the field of Theology.

For all of his forthrightness in the areas revelation, miracles, and Christ; Foster remained the purveyor of riddles. He specialized on the turn of a phrase, of rhetorical device. He is criticized for his ambiguity.¹¹⁴ This may have been because he "was ambivalent in his own theological position" by reason that he did not want to lose his ties to evangelical Protestantism all the while conceiving a new and more radical theology.¹¹⁵ Even if we judge Foster to be a moderate liberal, we would have to affirm his radical bent:

> Some of his radicalism can be excused as inconsistencies or tentativeness. He died before he had published a smooth and sanded theological product. However ambiguous and unsettled his theology seemed, he *was* exploring radical possibilities in his rejection

---

111. Peden, "The Chicago School (1906–1926) in American Religious Thought," 35.
112. Foster, *The Function of Religion*, 22.
113. Peden, "The Chicago School (1906–1926) in American Religious Thought," 42.
114. Koss, "The Development of Naturalism at the Divinity School of the University of Chicago," 13.
115. Koss, "The Development of Naturalism at the Divinity School of the University of Chicago," 15.

of personalism, his uncertainty in ontology and his inclination toward functionalism.[116]

The historical theologian can make a cogent argument that the secularism of the middle of the twentieth century, the sociocritical school, Death of God movement, Process theology, and many of the current trends in post-modern theological endeavors owe something to the thought and work of Foster. If they are not further developments upon the same theme, they have at least borrowed a few of his ideas. Foster's legacy is the orphaned theological children he brought into this world. They grew to maturity and we have withstood their legacy. Perhaps, as the excesses of life's trials accumulated they spent most of the inheritance Foster was to give to the next generation. Nevertheless, the family traits were passed on.

---

116. Koss, "The Development of Naturalism at the Divinity School of the University of Chicago," 44.

8

The Fundamentalist as Historian

The Civil War Histories of Clarence Macartney

MARK SIDWELL

HISTORY IS NOT NEUTRAL—or rather, historians are not. No matter how keenly a historian recognizes his or her own biases and attempts to correct them, no work of history can achieve objectivity. Rather than bemoan this fact, one may instead seize the opportunity it presents to examine how beliefs of historians are revealed in their works—how ideology shapes their histories. An intriguing and little studied example is Clarence Edward Noble Macartney (1879–1957), a historian with staunchly conservative Christian beliefs on his writing of history.

A Presbyterian minister, Macartney's reputation is as a master of the pulpit. As pastor of First Presbyterian Church in Paterson, New Jersey (1905–14); Arch Street Presbyterian Church in Philadelphia (1914–27); and finally First Presbyterian Church in Pittsburgh (1927–53), Macartney deservedly earned a reputation as one of the great pulpiteers in American history. His published sermons sold well and widely in his day, as did his guide to sermon preparation, *Preaching Without Notes*. Appropriately, *Preaching* magazine recognized Macartney in its list of the top ten preachers of the twentieth century.[1]

---

1. I have had the pleasure and privilege of knowing Dr. Priest since our days together in graduate school and through our constant interaction at conferences and meetings across the years. I have long appreciated his careful and thorough scholarship as a

Macartney also achieved a degree of fame as a controversialist in the Fundamentalist-Modernist controversy within the Presbyterian church. Listed with Macartney among the top ten preachers of the century was Harry Emerson Fosdick (1878–1969). Macartney's pursuit of the liberal Fosdick, which led to Fosdick's resignation from First Presbyterian Church of New York City, marked one of the triumphs of the conservative cause in the Presbyterian Church in the USA. At the same time, Macartney's election as moderator of the denomination in 1924 marked the crest of conservative efforts to reverse the spread of liberalism in the Presbyterian Church.[2] Macartney professed ambivalence about the label *Fundamentalist*, associating it with premillennialism, but his own staunch conservatism and his willingness "to contend for the faith" against theological Modernism placed him in the orbit of the Fundamentalist party.[3]

Yet Macartney was also a successful published historian.[4] He wrote a number of books on church history, local history of the Pittsburgh region, and notably books about the Civil War. Although little known today, these books sold reasonably well and contributed to Macartney's

---

historian but also his genuine burden to use his field of study in furthering Christian ministry. History is not a dry-as-dust subject to Jerry but the story of a sovereign God building His city. I chose this topic, in part, because I can think of few people who better exemplify the idea of "the Fundamentalist as historian" than Dr. Jerry Priest.

Michael Duduit, "The Ten Greatest Preachers of the Twentieth Century," *Preaching*, November/December 1999, 6–16.

2. On Macartney in the Presbyterian controversy, see Bradley J. Longfield, *The Presbyterian Controversy: Fundamentalists, Modernists, and Moderates* (New York: Oxford University Press, 1991) especially 104–27; C. Allyn Russell, *Voices of American Fundamentalism* (Philadelphia: Westminster, 1976) 190–211; and Mark Sidwell, "Clarence Macartney and the Presbyterian Controversy," *Biblical Viewpoint* 38, no. 1 (2004) 71–78, and no. 2, 75–82.

3. Macartney wrote of the label *Fundamentalist*, "It is a grand name, and the man who claims it certainly puts the burden of proof on those who differ from him," but added that because the name had become associated with premillennialism he did not use the term, for "we do not believe that an opinion, conviction or expectation as to the time of the second Epiphany of Christ is a fundamental of the Christian faith." Clarence Edward Macartney, *Shall Unbelief Win? A Reply to Dr. Fosdick* (Philadelphia: Wilbur Hanf, n.d.) 6. Macartney made a similar observation in his autobiography, *The Making of a Minister*, ed. J. Clyde Henry (Great Neck, NY: Channel, 1961) 184.

4. Apparently the only previous study of Macartney as a historian is Robert James Havlik, "The Lincoln Civil War Books by Clarence Edward Macartney: A Re-evaluation of the Works of a Popular Lincoln Author and Civil War Buff." *Lincoln Herald* 102, no. 1 (2000) 12–18. His article is primarily a listing of Macartney's Civil War histories that reviews the contents and significance of each book.

reputation, perhaps spreading his influence beyond his preaching ministry. Since Macartney was first a minister and an orthodox Protestant, the question is how his conservative theology affected his writing. How does a Fundamentalist write history?

Background of a Part-Time Historian

Macartney was born in Northwood, Ohio, where his father a was a professor at Geneva College, the school of the Reformed Presbyterian Church in North America, a group with its roots in the Scottish Covenanter tradition. When he was a year old the school moved (and the Macartney family with it) to Beaver Falls, Pennsylvania, where Macartney spent his early years. Macartney did his undergraduate studies at the University of Wisconsin. After graduating in 1901, he was at loose ends for a year, considering several career options, including that of history teacher. Believing himself called to the ministry, he enrolled at Princeton Theological Seminary in 1902, graduated three years later, and began his long association with the Presbyterian Church with his call to Paterson, New Jersey.

Asked when he first developed his interest in the Civil War, Macartney recalled that when he was a boy living at Geneva College, a visiting lecturer deeply impressed him with his discussions of Abraham Lincoln and the Civil War.[5] Macartney's father had been a conductor on the Underground Railroad in Ohio, which perhaps sparked some interest.[6] Macartney himself recalled reading during his boyhood "the stirring account of the Battle of Gettysburg" from an encyclopedia volume belonging to his father.[7]

His years at the University of Wisconsin further nourished a love for history, where he was a student during the tenure of Frederick Jackson Turner (1861–1932), the father of the profoundly influential frontier thesis of American history. Unfortunately, Macartney recalled, "I did not have a course under him for he was on leave of absence for part of the time when we were in college; but I got to know him well and he put me through my

---

5. G. Hall Todd, *He Being Dead Yet Speaketh: Tributes to Clarence Edward Noble Macartney* (Philadelphia?: n.p., 1979?) 11–12. Macartney Papers. Geneva College Archives, Geneva College, Beaver Falls, PA. (Hereafter "Macartney Papers.")

6. His father's association with the Underground Railroad is mentioned in "Address Delivered at the Funeral by Dr. George Kennedy," *In Memoriam: The Reverend J. L. McCartney, D.D. 1828–1911*, 9. Macartney Papers. Folder: Dr. J. L. McCartney, 1828–1911.

7. Macartney, *Making of a Minister*, 217.

oration on one occasion."[8] He did say that Charles Haskins, professor of medieval history at Wisconsin and perhaps the leading medievalist in the United States in his day, "opened to me the romance and thrill of history," and he also recalled fondly Carl Fish who lectured American history.[9] At Princeton he found the professor of church history, John DeWitt, "rather pompous." Yet allowing that DeWitt "was not equipped in a technical sense as are most professors in that field," Macartney thought that "he had something that technical research cannot bestow, and gave us most interesting lectures on the great epochs and commanding personalities of church history."[10] Even more influential was the assistant professor and successor to DeWitt, Lefferts Loetscher. Macartney described Loetscher as "scholarly and brilliant" and said he "did more than any other to open for me the thrill, romance and majesty of the long history of the Christian Church. This proved to be of the highest importance for me in my work as a minister."[11] These teachers and classes at Wisconsin and Princeton constituted Macartney's exposure to the discipline of history. He was not a novice, and his professors (such as Haskins, Fish, and Loetscher) were notable in their fields, but Macartney did not specialize in the discipline.

After he entered the pastorate, Macartney continued his historical researches, turning out a steady stream of articles and books, the first an unremarkable history of the First Presbyterian Church of Paterson, New Jersey, where he was pastor.[12] Some of Macartney's later books fall roughly into the category of church history, for instance, *The Minister's Son: A Record of His Achievements*, a short work on the accomplishments of the sons of ministers, and two books based on seminary lectures sketching famous preachers of the past.[13] He also wrote about secular topics, such as *Men*

---

8. "Look Backward—And Looking Forward," 3–4, an address by Macartney at the fiftieth anniversary of the University of Wisconsin class of 1901, June 16, 1951. Macartney Papers. Folder: L. A. Brunckhorst—Letter from (U. of Wisc.).

9. "Look Backward—And Looking Forward," 4.

10. Macartney, *The Making of a Minister*, 124. For the philosophy and approach to history of DeWitt, see Stephen H. Barnhart, "The Nineteenth-Century Church History Professors at Princeton Seminary: A Study in the Princeton Theology's Treatment of Church History" (PhD diss., Bob Jones University, 1986) 326–63.

11. Macartney, *The Making of a Minister*, 124.

12. *A History of the First Presbyterian Church of Paterson, New Jersey* (Paterson, NJ: First Presbyterian Church, n.d.). Available online http://www.archive.org/details/historyoffirstproomaca.

13. *The Minister's Son: A Record of His Achievements* (Philadelphia: Eakins, Palmer, and Harrar, 1917). Available online http://www.archive.org/details/

Who Missed It: Great Americans Who Missed the White House (1940), biographies of notable presidential losers.[14] A curious work is *The Bonapartes in America* (1939), which he co-wrote with Gordon Dorrance.[15] Here the authors traced in readable, if light, fashion the impact of the Bonaparte family on the United States, from Napoleon III's visit while in exile to the family that descended from the marriage of Jerome Bonaparte (Napoleon's youngest brother) to American Elizabeth Patterson.

After moving to Pittsburgh, Macartney took a keen interest in the history of that area, writing books on Pittsburgh, western Pennsylvania, and adjacent regions: *Not Far From Pittsburgh* (1936), *Right Here in Pittsburgh* (1937), and *Where the Rivers Meet* (1946).[16] These books contain sketches and articles on such topics as Johnny Appleseed, Stephen Foster, the Johnstown flood, Abraham Lincoln's visit to Pittsburgh, and the Homestead strike. Macartney's sister noted that he had served as a reporter for a Beaver Falls newspaper right after he graduated from college, and she thought this experience "was helpful in developing certain aspects of his style. Many passages in his historical books have the vividness of first-class reporting."[17] This journalistic flavor is clearly evident in his regional histories.

Of central interest to this study are Macartney's seven books on the Civil War: *Lincoln and His Generals* (1925), *Highways and Byways of the Civil War* (1926), *Lincoln and His Cabinet* (1931), *Little Mac: The Life of General George B. McClellan* (1940), *Lincoln and the Bible* (1949), *Grant and His Generals* (1953), and *Mr. Lincoln's Admirals* (1956).[18] Macartney

---

ministerssonrecooomacarich; he dedicated the book to Woodrow Wilson, the son of a minister, currently occupying the White House. The works on noted preachers were *The Sons of Thunder: Pulpit Power of the Past* (New York: Revell, 1929), based on the L. P. Stone Lectures he delivered at Princeton in 1928, and *Six Kings of the American Pulpit* (Philadelphia: Westminster, 1942), based on Macartney's Smythe lectures at Columbia Theological Seminary of 1939.

14. *Men Who Missed It: Great Americans Who Missed the White House* (Philadelphia: Dorrance, 1940).

15. *The Bonapartes in America* (Philadelphia: Dorrance, 1939).

16. *Not Far From Pittsburgh* (Pittsburgh: Gibson, 1936), *Right Here in Pittsburgh* (Pittsburgh: Gibson, 1937), *Where the Rivers Meet* (Pittsburgh: Gibson, 1946).

17. Wilhemina Guerard, "Clarence Macartney: Biographical Notes," 33 (typescript). Macartney Papers.

18. *Lincoln and His Generals* (Philadelphia: Dorrance, 1925); *Highways and Byways of the Civil War* (Philadelphia: Dorrance, 1926), a second edition was published in Pittsburgh by Gibson Press in 1938 and all quotations come from the second edition; *Lincoln and His Cabinet* (New York: Charles Scribner's Sons, 1931); *Little Mac: The Life of General*

published several of these through the Dorrance Company, a vanity press based in Philadelphia. The profits appear to have been sufficient to keep Macartney working through Dorrance. Other books, however, attracted the attention of major publishers (Scribner's, Funk and Wagnalls), and one Dorrance publication, *Lincoln and His Generals*, was later reprinted by another publisher.[19]

Approach to History

As an amateur, popular historian, Clarence Macartney professed no explicit philosophy of history. Likely for this reason, he showed no influence of a particular school of interpretation.[20] One potential influence on his work, however, is Common Sense Realism, a school of philosophy associated with Thomas Reid (1710–96), and other figures in the Scottish Enlightenment.[21] Historians have highlighted the influence of Common Sense Realism on American intellectual history, particularly in religion, in the late eighteenth and nineteenth centuries.[22] Scottish-born John Witherspoon (1723–94), introduced the approach during his presidency of Princeton College, and it was in the Princeton tradition (of which Macartney was an heir) that the

---

George B. McClellan (Philadelphia: Dorrance, 1940); *Lincoln and the Bible* (New York: Abingdon-Cokesbury, 1949); *Grant and His Generals* (New York: McBride Company, 1953); *Mr. Lincoln's Admirals* (New York: Funk & Wagnalls, 1956).

19. Reprinted by Books for Libraries (Freeport, NY) in 1970.

20. Because Macartney studied at Wisconsin when Frederick Jackson Turner was in residence (although he took no classes from Turner), one is tempted to look for traces in Macartney of the frontier thesis, Turner's argument that the presence of the frontier explains the character of American history, notably the growth of democracy. In Macartney's regional histories he does show a little of the Turner frontier flavor, as in the dedication of *Not Far from Pittsburgh* "to the memory of men of iron and faith, who with rifle, axe, and psalm book conquered a wilderness." But Macartney's writings display no consistent development of this concept.

21. For an introduction to and analysis of Common Sense Realism, see Nicholas Wolterstorff, *Thomas Reid and the Story of Epistemology* (Cambridge: Cambridge University Press, 2001).

22. The pioneer work in tracing the influence of Common Sense Realism in American thought is Sidney Ahlstrom, "The Scottish Philosophy and American Theology," *Church History* 24 (1955) 257–72. For a fuller study, see Theodore Dwight Bozeman, *Protestants in an Age of Science: The Baconian Ideal and Antebellum American Religious Thought* (Chapel Hill: University of North Carolina Press, 1977). I would like to thank Ronald Wells for suggesting to me the framework of Common Sense Realism as a potential avenue to Macartney's thought.

philosophy made a lasting impact.[23] In brief, Common Sense Realism held against other schools that humans have direct acquaintance with reality rather than having such acquaintance mediated through ideas or interpretations. This fact renders knowledge widely accessible and also assumes a consistency of how individuals view that knowledge. Closely tied to this view of epistemology is the idea of "Baconian induction," that knowledge is the gathering and organizing of data provided by the senses.

Macartney's writings provide reason to believe that Common Sense Realism influenced him. In *Christianity and Common Sense* (1927), an apologetic for Christianity, Macartney wrote:

> But anything that may be said in behalf of Christianity from the standpoint of common sense has a universal appeal, for all men are gifted with a degree of common sense, and thus are qualified to pass upon any evidence that may be advanced from that source. Nor is any sensible person prejudiced against the evidence of common sense.[24]

Common sense serves as a guide to what is revealed, not as a source of wisdom itself. Macartney denied "that man's unaided reason could ever have discovered the truths of Christianity without the revelation, but only that since the laws of Christianity have been revealed, man's common sense approves and confirms those laws."[25] He wrote, "If an uneducated man were to tell you what his common sense had to say about the Hittites... you might be justified in telling him that his common sense was only nonsense. These are questions for scholars to decide. All that common sense can do is to pass on the evidence."[26]

As an orthodox Calvinist, Macartney professed a strong belief in Providence, what he called "the majestic doctrine of God in history." This assertion "means that the supreme actor on the stage of history is God; and the great epochs, the great nations, and the great personalities are but the

---

23. It is worth noting, however, that Barnhart sees John DeWitt, Macartney's professor of church history at Princeton, as marking a shift from Common Sense Realism in Princeton's church history program. Under the influence of H. B. Smith and W. G. T. Shedd of Union Seminary, DeWitt moved toward an organic, developmental view of history owing a debt to continental trends in historical studies. See Barnhart, 329–30.

24. Clarence Edward Macartney, *Christianity and Common Sense: A Dialogue of Faith* (Chicago: John C. Winston Company, 1927) vi.

25. Macartney, *Christianity and Common Sense*, viii.

26. Macartney, *Christianity and Common Sense*, 216–17.

brief embodiment and the transient realization of his eternal purpose."[27] He rejected the idea of tracing Providence only in those circumstances that are pleasing to the observer, pointing out that one of the supreme examples of divine Providence is also one of the most terrible, the crucifixion of Christ.[28] Macartney also viewed history as didactic, as having value in teaching humans practical examples from the past as a guide. Making a contrast with prophecy, he wrote, "Philosophers and historians do not attempt to foretell the future. They deal with the past and draw what lessons they can for the future, but they make no attempt to lift the veil that hides tomorrow."[29] Note also that Macartney referred to learning the "romance" and "thrill" of history in college. Although the image is hardly original with him, one notes his description of the leaders in the Civil War as "the chief actors of the drama."[30] He believed that history—really *good* history—should pulse with drama, not simply to entertain but to edify. And the director of that drama was God.

Writing About the Civil War

Clarence Macartney's outlook on the Civil War was fundamentally pro-Union. In *Christianity and Common Sense* Macartney's narrator reflects on the Civil War that "there were good men on both sides [of the Civil War], and both sides thought they were right. But now it is possible for all to look back and see how that conflict was only one short chapter in the long struggle between good and evil."[31] There is no reason to think

27. "God in History," in *The Man Who Forgot and Other Sermons on Bible Characters* (New York: Abingdon, 1956) 25. This sermon focuses on Cyrus the Great as an example of God's working in history.

28. "God in History," 26, 28–29.

29. *The Faith Once Delivered* (New York: Abingdon-Cokesbury, 1952) 51.

30. *Highways and Byways*, 295.

31. *Christianity and Common Sense*, 66. Edith W. Thompson, an assistant secretary to Macartney recalled, "He loved Abraham Lincoln.... Dr. Macartney's sympathies lay, of course, with the Union; but he had great admiration for Robert E. Lee. His sympathies lay with the slaves and the freed blacks after the War." Edith W. Thompson, "Memories of Dr. Clarence Edward Macartney" (typescript) June 15, 1984, 2. Macartney Papers. Folder: In Memoriam Dr. Clarence E. Macartney. It is also worth observing that in a collection of illustrations from Macartney's sermons, there are about seventy-five illustrations from Civil War, the large majority of them about the Union side with a healthy percentage of these dealing with Abraham Lincoln. *Macartney's Illustrations* (New York: Abingdon-Cokesbury, 1945).

Macartney's personal opinion was any different. As for the cause of the war, he wrote, "The chief cause of the war was slavery, but the occasion of it was secession."[32] He saw a straightforward moral question at the center of the war, although he extended charity toward those on the other side. Borrowing from Lincoln, he wrote, "The North thought slavery was wrong; the South thought it was right."[33] Furthermore, he saw the war, terrible as it was, as purifying and redeeming the nation. He declared, for example, that when Joseph Johnston surrendered to Sherman to end the war, "the nation stood regenerated."[34]

Macartney researched his works carefully and thoroughly. Part of this research was personal. He visited numerous Civil War sites, describing, for example, a trip on horseback through the Wilderness in northern Virginia (a trip especially memorable to Macartney because he fell off his horse and broke his arm).[35] He likewise referred to other occasions, such as a trip to the Pigeon Creek Baptist Church in Indiana that young Lincoln attended.[36] He intended his *Highways and Byways of the Civil War* in part to serve as a guide book for such sites. Even more vital were Macartney's encounters with veterans. In the 1950s he recalled when he first started writing about the war, he could still speak with surviving veterans, mentioning particularly how he enjoyed attending the fiftieth anniversary of the Battle of Gettysburg, sitting among the survivors and listening to them recount their stories.[37]

The meat of his research, however, was documentary. Macartney avoided the pitfall so common to amateur historians of relying on secondary literature. Indeed, one criticism of his work is that he did little to engage the literature—to interact with, or even show an awareness of, the work of other historians of the Civil War. The reverse of that lack of engagement was Macartney's dependence on primary sources.[38] He showed a wide

32. *Little Mac*, 40.
33. *Little Mac*, 42–43.
34. *Highways and Byways*, 285.
35. *The Making of a Minister*, 172–73. His sister also recounts this story. "Clarence Macartney: Biographical Notes," 48–49. Macartney advised ministers to plan their vacations so that they might be profitable and not simply a diversion. "Many of my own vacations," he wrote, "were spent following in the footsteps of the Apostle Paul, and many others traversing the battlefields of the Civil War." *Making of a Minister*, 162.
36. *Macartney's Illustrations*, 31.
37. *Grant and His Generals*, xiv. See also *Macartney's Illustrations*, 110.
38. His "Authorities" section for *Lincoln and His Cabinet* (v–ix) does list a number of

knowledge of published primary materials (the *Official Records*, memoirs, and collections of letters), but beyond that Macartney dug into unpublished sources and delighted in tracking down new ones. A good example is his description of "Sources and Authorities" in *Grant and His Generals*.[39] Macartney said he visited libraries "from the Vermont State Historical Library at Montpelier, to the Huntington Library in California," as well as the Library of Congress. He uncovered manuscript sources such as an unpublished biography of John A. McClernand (1812–1900), and the previously little used papers of William F. ("Baldy") Smith (1824–1903), including an unpublished autobiography.[40] Macartney also surveyed newspapers and magazines of the Civil War period. Robert James Havlik notes that the "Authorities" section of Macartney's *Highways and Byways of the Civil War* aptly summarizes Macartney's approach to research—his search through the sources joined to his trips to the sites he wrote about.[41]

Unfortunately, Macartney's footnoting was eccentric. His use of citations varied from book to book. In *Lincoln and His Generals*, there was little footnoting. In *Lincoln and His Cabinet*, he footnoted thoroughly. In *Grant and His Generals*, he apparently footnoted only what did not come from primary sources.[42] His limited use of footnotes probably encouraged him to include minor material in the text, such as calculations on the percentage of naval officers who went over to the Confederacy.[43] In most of Macartney's books, tracing his quotations can be frustrating.

---

secondary works, but the list is still weighted heavily to primary sources. In his papers are extensive lists of manuscript collections concerning Civil War generals. See Macartney Papers. Folder: Civil War Manuscripts.

39. *Grant and His Generals*, xii–xiv.

40. Reviewers of *Grant and His Generals* noted particularly the original contribution of the chapter on Baldy Smith, because Macartney was the first to have access to Smith's unfinished autobiography and his papers and letters. See John B. Barrett, Review of *Grant and His Generals*, *North Carolina Historical Review* 31 (1954) 598–99. Another reviewer calls the chapter on Smith "the most important chapter in the book" because of Macartney's use of these resources. Richard O'Connor, Review of *Grant and His Generals*, *American Historical Review* 59 (1954) 394.

41. See Havlik, "The Lincoln Civil War Books by Clarence Edward Macartney," 14. Havlik quotes the entire "Authorities" section (two paragraphs) of *Highways and Byways*, 295, to illustrate.

42. *Mr. Lincoln's Admirals* used few footnotes but instead listed the pages relevant to the topics with each entry in the bibliography (318–19).

43. *Mr. Lincoln's Admirals*, 35–36.

Yet Macartney did not quote sources naïvely. While researching *Lincoln and the Bible*, he encountered the reminiscences of the Canadian Charles Chiniquy (1809–99), about his dealings with Lincoln. A Catholic priest who later left the Roman Church and became a leading anti-Catholic polemicist, Chiniquy related several stories and conversations he allegedly had with Lincoln in Illinois and later in the White House. In attempting to gauge Chiniquy's reliability, Macartney wrote to James G. Randall at the University of Illinois, who replied with sources that Macartney might consult. Macartney seems to have taken Randall's advice to heart. Although he quoted from Chiniquy without qualification, his footnote on the background of Chiniquy's relationship to Lincoln is restrained and factual, not the romanticized account that Chiniquy offered in his memoir *Fifty Years in the Church of Rome*.[44]

An even better example of Macartney's study of his sources is the saga of the "sleeping sentinel." The account concerned Private William Scott of the Third Vermont Regiment who was sentenced to be shot for sleeping on duty in the fall of 1861. According to the popular account, Lincoln personally intervened to save Scott, even making a whirlwind visit to army headquarters to make sure the pardon was applied. Macartney first related this story in *Little Mac*, though he admitted that no such pardon existed in official records.[45] After further research, however, Macartney rejected the tale based on indications in Baldy Smith's papers that the sentencing and last-minute pardon were a put-up job to promote discipline by making an example of Scott. Private Scott was indeed pardoned at the last moment, but by McClellan, not Lincoln, who had nothing to do with the event, Macartney concluded. After further study, Macartney asserted that the traditional story was "not credible," and he published a corrected version in *Grant and His Generals*.[46]

---

44. J. G. Randall to Clarence Macartney June 16, 1948. Macartney Papers. Folder: Lincoln and the Bible. Randall said he knew little about Chiniquy but mentioned letters from Chiniquy to Lincoln housed in the Library of Congress as well as an article by Carl Russell Fish on Lincoln and Catholicism and a critical discussion of Chiniquy in Beveridge's biography of Lincoln. See *Lincoln and the Bible*, 92–96. For more on the relation of Chiniquy to Lincoln, see Joseph George Jr., "The Lincoln Writings of Charles P. T. Chiniquy," *Journal of the Illinois Historical Society* 69 (1976) 17–25.

45. *Little Mac*, 165–66. Macartney cited L. E. Chittenden, *Recollections of President Lincoln and His Administration* (New York: Harper & Brothers, 1901), as the source for the story.

46. Macartney Papers. Folder: "New Light on the Sleeping Sentinel" by Clarence Macartney. *Grant and His Generals*, 190–92. Ironically, documents uncovered in the late

Writing a "Christian" History?

The question naturally arises of how "Christian" was the version of history written by the Presbyterian minister. Admittedly, some inclusions may surprise readers who think of Macartney as a "Fundamentalist historian." For instance, he quoted profanity numerous times and advocated stern war measures that may seem out of character for a minister, such as suggesting that "a little wise and prompt hanging upon the trees at the beginning of the war would have shortened the war and reduced its sorrows and its horrors."[47]

On the whole, however, Macartney's religious beliefs colored his writing. A prominent example is Macartney's appeals to Providence. A prime instance, not only for its content but also for its almost biblical language, is Macartney's comment on a conversation he had with a Confederate veteran of the Battle of Shiloh. Quoting the veteran as wishing "if only" General Beauregard had not given the order to cease fire at the end of the first day of fighting, Macartney essentially moved from writing to preaching:

> Ah, my fine veteran, still so straight and erect, thy grey eyes lighting with ardor once more as thou dost speak of that spring day fight in the woods of Shiloh, how many battles have been lost by an "if." "*If* it had not rained the night before Waterloo." "*If* Lee's orders to Jackson in the Antietam campaign had not been found wrapped about cigars." "*If* Ahasuerhas had been able to sleep on that night when ferocious Haman was plotting for the annihilation of the Jews." Knowest thou not, my fine old veteran, after the lapse of more than half a century almost as thou dost tell me of the fatal order that lost the battle and lost the cause in the woods on the banks of the Tennessee, knowest thou not that history is made of "ifs," but that back of those "ifs" stands the eternal purpose of One with whom there is no variableness, neither shadow of turning, and that the great nations, the great empires, and the great battles, are but the brief embodiment or the transient realization of His desires?[48]

---

twentieth century indicate Lincoln may have indeed had a hand in the pardon, even to the point of visiting army headquarters, although not in the dramatic fashion portrayed in the original story. See William Lee Miller, *President Lincoln: The Duty of a Statesman* (New York: Knopf, 2008) 328–31.

47. For examples of profanity from John A. Logan at Belmont, William T. Sherman, and even of Lincoln himself, see *Grant and His Generals*, 101, 295, and *Lincoln and His Generals*, 79, respectively. For the "hanging" comment, see *Lincoln and His Cabinet*, 41.

48. *Highways and Byways*, 102. The rather Victorian prose of this passage is not

Once for All Delivered to the Saints

As this paragraph shows, the concept of historical "counterfactuals" (the "what ifs" of history) did not appeal to Macartney, at least in theory. "History is never made with an *If*," he declared; "neither can it be written with an *If*." However, immediately thereafter he observed that if Baldy Smith had remained on Grant's staff, the Union army would have avoided disasters such as Cold Harbor.[49] Likewise Macartney inconsistently wrote, "It is vain to attempt to write history with an IF. But the student of that period of American history will sometimes wonder if, during the decade of 1850 to 1860, a great and far-seeing statesman might not have saved the nation from civil war."[50]

In invoking Providence, Macartney usually did not refer to smaller details—the storm that saved a regiment or the bullet halted by a Bible in the pocket. Normally, he referred to Providence only as part of the overall picture. He was willing to speculate on the ways of God only in generalizations about the larger results. Thus he wrote, "Here lies buried the Confederacy, 'One of those causes which pleased noble spirits, but did not please destiny.'"[51] Commenting on James Longstreet's statement that if the Federal government had just left the Southern states alone, they would have come back, Macartney wrote, "But He who decrees the destinies of men and nations had determined otherwise, for not only was the Union to be preserved and restored, but the whole nation was to drink a cup of woe due to those by whom the offense of slavery had come."[52] Writing of Lincoln's hesitance to issue the Emancipation Proclamation, Macartney said, "But God decreed otherwise. Lincoln's explanation was that he had not controlled events, but that events had controlled him. The great Controller of human affairs had

---

characteristic of the whole of work.

49. *Grant and His Generals*, 219.

50. *Lincoln and His Cabinet*, 3. One should note that in *Men Who Missed It*, his history of presidential losers, Macartney often resorted to "ifs" to highlight their failure: if Burr had supported Jefferson for president in 1800 (11); if Clay had not written his letter on the annexation of Texas (20); if Douglas had stood against slavery on moral grounds (58); if McClellan had supported Lincoln in 1863 (62, 65–66); if S. T. Burchard had not referred to "Rum, Romanism, and Rebellion" during James G. Blaine's campaign (91–92); if Charles Evans Hughes had never visited California (114, 118–19). Note also his sermon on the word *if*: "The Weakest Word," in *The Greatest Words in the Bible and in Human Speech* (Nashville: Cokesbury, 1938) 106–17.

51. *Highways and Byways*, 294.

52. *Lincoln and His Generals*, 18. Macartney duplicated this passage in *Little Mac*, 73.

decreed that the slaves should be free, and that the hand which signed the writ of their emancipation should be that of Abraham Lincoln."[53]

These quotations sound of divine sovereignty and even divine judgment. But Macartney also saw Christianity as a force within history, even when those at the center of events did not recognize this fact. An example is the article he wrote on abolitionist Arthur B. Bradford. A Presbyterian minister, Bradford founded the pro-abolition Free Presbyterian Church before the Civil War, because he thought the mainline Presbyterian Church was not militant enough over the issue. Bradford eventually left the ministry and abandoned Christianity altogether, becoming a vocal free thinker and critic of Christianity. Rebuking Bradford's appeal to paganism and "natural religion" as superior to Christianity, Macartney waxed eloquent on Christianity's effect on history:

> No, Arthur Bradford, you were greatly mistaken! You apparently failed to note that the Pagan religion, and what you called "Natural" religion, did nothing for the outcast and the slave. Had you forgotten what Paul wrote when he sent the runaway slave, Onesimus, back to his master, Philemon, at Colosse, and told him to receive him back, "not now as a slave, but above a slave, a brother beloved"? There the axe was laid to the root of the tree of human slavery; and it was the Gospel of Jesus Christ which, in your hands, and in the hands of your fellow Abolitionists, was the weapon of truth and justice and love for man which destroyed slavery in America.[54]

The Bible also played a role in Macartney's account of history. In *Lincoln and the Bible*, Macartney said that he had found seventy-seven clear quotations from or allusions to the Bible in Lincoln's speeches and conversations. He contrasted Lincoln's day with his own, asserting that when Lincoln alluded to the Bible most people would grasp the allusions without explanation.[55] Yet Macartney himself constantly alluded to the Scriptures in his Civil War histories with the evident expectation that his readers would recognize the references. Thus he likened emergence of a spring at Andersonville prison camp with the water coming forth from the stone as a

---

53. *Lincoln and His Cabinet*, 243.

54. "'Buttonwood' and a Great Abolitionist," *Princeton Seminary Bulletin* 44, No. 3, (1950) 28. Available online http://commons.ptsem.edu/id/princetonseminar4431prin-dmd007.

55. *Lincoln and the Bible*, 6–7.

result of Moses' rod.[56] Noting General Joseph Hooker's boast before Chancellorsville that "God Almighty could not prevent him from destroying the Confederate Army," Macartney replied, "But let not him that girdeth on his harness boast himself as he that putteth it off."[57] On General Benjamin Butler and his ring of informers in New Orleans, Macartney said, "As it was in the day of Benhadad and Elisha, the words spoken in the bedchamber were soon repeated to Butler."[58] Prior to Lincoln's inauguration "people were turning toward Springfield and asking: 'Watchman, what of the night?'"[59] Macartney likened Montgomery Blair of Lincoln's cabinet to Ishmael: "He shall be as a wild-ass among men; his hand shall be against every man, and every man's hand against him; and he shall dwell in the presence of all his brethren."[60] Generals Sherman, Sheridan, and McPherson resembled "the 'first three' of David's mighty men."[61] He even borrowed the language of Christ's selecting His disciples when he titled the prologue to his work on Lincoln's cabinet "Of Them He Chose Seven."[62] These references flow unaffectedly from Macartney with no trace of self-consciousness.

Macartney's sympathies emerge clearly in his descriptions of men he believed genuine Christians. He almost shone when portraying those with a strong Christian testimony, such Andrew Hull Foote (1806–63), commander of the Union gunboat fleet in the West.[63] He incidentally wove observations about piety into his biographies. Thus Gideon Welles was "a deeply religious man and consistent church member," Admiral Farragut prayed before going into Mobile Bay, and William Cushing asked his mother to pray for him before undertaking the dangerous attempt to blow up the Confederate ram *Albemarle*.[64] Macartney believed firmly in the sincerity and religious character of John Brown, even describing him as a man who died a "vicarious death" on behalf of Blacks.[65] Macartney never wrote

---

56. *Highways and Byways*, 246. Cf. Exod 17:6.

57. *Little Mac*, 316. Cf. 1 Kgs 20:11.

58. *Lincoln and His Generals*, 54. Cf. 2 Kgs 6:12.

59. *Lincoln and His Cabinet*, 9. Cf. Isa 21:11.

60. *Lincoln and His Cabinet*, 285. Cf. Gen 16:12.

61. *Grant and His Generals*, xi. Cf. 2 Sam 23:8–17.

62. *Lincoln and His Cabinet*, xi. Cf. Luke 6:13.

63. *Mr. Lincoln's Admirals*, 78–115. Macartney began this portrait by discussing the "saints" in the army and navy, 78–79.

64. *Mr. Lincoln's Admirals*, 4, 69, 210, respectively.

65. *Christianity and Common Sense*, 152, 154. Brown impressed Macartney so deeply

a full sketch of General Oliver O. Howard (1830–1909), widely known as the Union's "Christian General," but he used him as a pattern, as in likening General James McPherson to Howard in being "total abstainer and an earnest Christian."[66]

Macartney admired no figure from the Civil War more than Abraham Lincoln. He quoted Edward Bates' description of Lincoln "very near being a perfect man" as "the nearest to history's verdict" about him.[67] He viewed Lincoln in a biblical framework, even borrowing Scriptural language for Christ to describe the president as "a man of sorrows and acquainted with grief."[68] The vexed question of Lincoln's religious faith therefore challenged him, and he took up that challenge in *Lincoln and the Bible*.

The shortest of his Civil War books, *Lincoln and the Bible* was also the most overtly religious of Macartney's Civil War publications, published in fact through a religious press (Abingdon-Cokesbury). Despite the book's brevity and focus, Macartney competently surveyed major data about Lincoln's religious beliefs. He dealt with evidence of Lincoln's early skepticism, his references to God (especially in the war years), and above all his references to the Bible. Although the book is more devotional than his other histories, Macartney did take time to scrutinize the evidence. For example, he carefully examined the story of Lincoln's "infidel book," a writing by Lincoln in his years in New Salem, Illinois, in which he allegedly attacked Christian doctrine. As the story goes, Lincoln destroyed the work so that it would not hinder his political career. While not completely discounting the story, Macartney noted that the story had been published by a political opponent and was at best a secondhand account.[69] Macartney highlighted any evidence of religious interest by Lincoln in his Civil War speeches, from

---

that he wrote a play about Brown, "John Brown: A Tragedy in Three Acts," unpublished but found in the Macartney Papers. Folder: John Brown.

66. *Grant and His Generals*, 64. Because he focused on the Union, Macartney did little with the Confederacy's Christian heroes, notably Robert E. Lee and Stonewall Jackson. A rare negative note contrasted Jackson with Union General George Thomas. Describing how the sisters of the Virginian Thomas disowned him for siding with the Union, Macartney commented: "This is in striking contrast with the attitude of Stonewall Jackson's sister, who characterized her brother as 'a moral coward' because, being opposed to both slavery and secession, he nevertheless fought with the Confederate Army." Macartney based this statement on secondhand evidence from a West Virginia lawyer who knew Jackson's sister in his earlier years. *Grant and His Generals*, 6.

67. *Lincoln and His Cabinet*, 82.
68. *Lincoln and His Generals*, 221.
69. *Lincoln and the Bible*, 18–20.

his meditations on the divine will to his second inaugural address. Perhaps only in his conclusion did he allow his faith to trump his evidence as he admitted a lack of reference in Lincoln concerning "a consciousness of sin and a trust in the atoning and redeeming work of Christ on the cross," but added, "But signs are not wanting that he was on his way to make a public confession of his faith in Christ when the assassin's bullet put an end to his probation."[70] The idea of "Lincoln the Christian" was at least a concept that Macartney yearned to believe.

Evaluation

Clarence Macartney's Civil War books seem to have sold well and earned a degree of respect in his own day. Contemporary reviewers noted the works, often favorably, but not uniformly so. A typical reviewer writing in *America* gave a mixed review to *Mr. Lincoln's Admirals*. He liked some chapters, although not those on Du Pont and Dahlgren, but criticized Macartney for not engaging the overall picture of the naval war.[71] By contrast, Richard O'Connor in the *American Historical Review* called *Grant and His Generals* "a solid historical work, bulwarked with scholarship and written with a commendable depth of understanding."[72] James Randall told Macartney, "Knowing the high quality of your previous writing I am sure that your forthcoming Lincoln and the Bible will be a most valuable and readable work"—although this comment may be simple professional courtesy.[73] Since Macartney's death, notices have been far fewer, although Havlik expressed appreciation of Macartney's work, saying for example that Lincoln and the Bible "has had and will continue to have a long life in the field of Lincolniana."[74]

Generally speaking, Macartney interacted little with contemporary scholarship. Occasionally one finds notes that reflect historical debates.

---

70. *Lincoln and the Bible*, 39–40.

71. *America*, 1 September 1956, 507. Macartney Papers. Folder: Reviews of Dr. McCartney's [sic] Books.

72. O'Connor, 394. He also recognized Macartney's past work in having "been engaged for forty years in studying and writing about the American Civil War."

73. J. G. Randall to Clarence Macartney, June 16, 1948. Macartney Papers. Folder: Lincoln and the Bible. Macartney apparently collected any and all reviews (no matter how brief) and at one point engaged Literary Clipping Service of Walton, New York, to track these.

74. Havlik, "The Lincoln Civil War Books by Clarence Edward Macartney," 17.

Macartney, for example, appeared to reply to James Randall's argument that the Civil War was a "needless war" caused by a "blundering generation" of extremists on both sides. Macartney rejected the idea "that the Civil War was brought on by a few irresponsible political firebrands, North and South." As evidence he cited parallel sermons by Henry Ward Beecher (1813–87), of Brooklyn and Benjamin Morgan Palmer (1818–1902), of New Orleans, both of whom were "mainstream" for their regions, and noted that the two sermons (both delivered on Thanksgiving Day, 1860) both claimed divine approval for their respective causes.[75]

One should not dismiss Macartney simply because he was not a professional historian. The field of Civil War writing as much as any genre demonstrates significant contributions of "talented amateurs." One need look no farther than Douglas Southall Freeman's studies of Robert E. Lee, Bruce Catton's numerous bestsellers on the war, and Shelby Foote's three-volume narrative to see that non-professionals have contributed richly. But Macartney's books do lack the weight that professionals often bring to the field. A good point of comparison is Macartney's *Lincoln and His Generals* and the book of the same title by T. Harry Williams.[76] Macartney's book is a series of biographical sketches linked by reference to Lincoln's relations with each figure. Williams' book is an integrated narrative focusing on Lincoln as a war president through his interaction with his generals. Williams goes deeper in analyzing relationships and tying his account to the overall framework of the war. Macartney's book is good; Williams' is better.

Still it is possible to fit Macartney's work into the historiography of the Civil War. Macartney showed many affinities to what Thomas Pressley labeled the "nationalist tradition" that flourished in the late nineteenth and early twentieth centuries,[77] a school of interpreters who stressed national reconciliation and downplayed regional prejudice. They generally saw the preservation of the Union and the abolition of slavery as benefits but were willing to respect the sincere beliefs of southerners in fighting the war. Pressley noted the popularity in this approach of the "cult of Lincoln and Lee" in which those two men were seen to represent the best

---

75. *Little Mac*, 42–43. Elsewhere, Macartney noted the sermon by Palmer in particular and said, "Anyone who takes the trouble to read this powerful, amazing, and eloquent sermon will be delivered from the illusion that the Civil War was brought on by a few irresponsible firebrands, North and South." *Lincoln and His Cabinet*, 14.

76. T. Harry Williams, *Lincoln and His Generals* (New York: Alfred A. Knopf, 1952).

77. Thomas J. Pressley, *Americans Interpret Their Civil War* (New York: Free Press, 1962) 221–26.

of motives on both sides. Certainly many of the emphases of this nationalist tradition were present in Macartney, and Macartney clearly had little interest in the more technical economic and social aspects of the war, which gained prominence during his lifetime. Writing in 1940 Macartney sounded this note of reconciliation by observing that in the years since the war, "passions have subsided, animosities have cooled, and reconciliations then unthinkable have taken place. The statues of Lee and Davis adorn the halls of the Capitol of the nation whose very existence their armies once threatened; and in two foreign wars the sons and grandsons of the men who followed Lee and McClellan have marched and fought side by side under the old flag."[78]

One of the few points at which Macartney plunged into a controversy (perhaps unintentionally) was the career of General George McClellan (1826–85), the subject of Macartney's only complete biography. The book is on the whole very favorable to the much-criticized Union commander. McClellan's son wrote to Macartney after its publication that Little Mac was "by far the fairest, the most objective, and the most sympathetic life of McClellan that I have read," and said it was a "great satisfaction to find a historian of high repute and standing doing him justice."[79] It is unlikely that the majority of McClellan studies pleased his son so well. Writers of what has been called the "Unionist" approach—from Lincoln's secretaries John Nicolay and John Hay to T. Harry Williams and Bruce Catton—have dismissed McClellan as incompetent, insubordinate, and generally an unpleasant person.[80] Macartney, by contrast, agreed with Robert E. Lee in considering McClellan the best of the Union commanders. In this case, Macartney's dissent from the majority opinion was likely not a conscious engagement with other historians, but his approach does stand in marked contrast. Unfortunately, Macartney's dissent does not seem to have won him much notice. Professional historians writing about McClellan have taken little note of Macartney, as in Warren Hassler's dismissal of

78. *Little Mac*, vi. Note also Macartney's citation of the irenic closing words of Grant's *Memoirs* in *Macartney's Illustrations*, 12.

79. George McClellan to Clarence Macartney, April 2, 1940. Macartney Papers. Folder: Books Reviews–McClellan–Little Mac.

80. See Joseph L. Harsh, "On the McClellan-Go-Round," *Civil War History* 19 (1973) 101–21; and Thomas J. Rowland, *George B. McClellan and Civil War History: In the Shadow of Grant and Sherman* (Kent, OH: Kent State University Press, 1998).

Macartney as "undocumented," "rather thin in parts, and with a number of grave defects."[81]

Stylistically, Macartney was a good writer. The same talents of communication he honed in the pulpit he displayed in his books. His writing was clear, although he could veer toward pretentiousness in striving for an exalted tone in some passages. He sometimes lapsed into a hortatory style unlikely to appeal to readers in the twenty-first century, but Macartney generally strove for an accessible style that would appeal to the common reader. "Slowly but surely," he wrote, "writers of history are escaping from the bondage of convention, and the idea that history must be heavy, dull and much documented." He cited as an example the *Dictionary of American Biography*, in which the "authors of the various articles have even dared to embellish and illuminate their accounts with anecdotes and conversations."[82]

Macartney's narratives were a little uneven. Most of his works (including those on topics outside the Civil War) were episodic, featuring chapters either unrelated or only loosely related to each other. Even his themed histories such as *Lincoln and His Generals* or *Grant and His Generals* were fundamentally a series of connected short biographies resembling his numerous sermon books that contained a series of messages based on an overarching theme. Only *Little Mac*, his biography of McClellan, was a single narrative, but it was less unified than it might have been, as Macartney digressed into side issues. *Lincoln and His Cabinet* is an example of Macartney's approach at its best. The personality of Lincoln more closely united the sketches of the cabinet members. Furthermore, Macartney often provoked dramatic interest in narratives such as the debate over Fort Sumter or the circumstances behind the issuing of the Emancipation Proclamation.

In *Lincoln and His Generals*, *Lincoln and His Cabinet*, and *Grant and His Generals*, the nature of the central figure (Lincoln or Grant) seems to shift with the perspective of each subordinate discussed. Criticism of Lincoln or Grant moves quickly—sometimes in the same chapter—to praise. The result is uneven characterization. It is sometimes difficult to determine Macartney's opinion even within individual portraits. An example is the sketch of Benjamin Butler (1893), in *Grant and His Generals*. Macartney

---

81. Warren W. Hassler, Jr., *General George McClellan: Shield of the Union* (Baton Rouge: Louisiana State University Press, 1957) 338. Harsh, "On the McClellan-Go-Round," refers in passing to "Clarence Macartney's thin essay" (103). Rowland mentions *Little Mac* in a footnote but gets the publisher wrong (196).

82. *Right Here in Pittsburgh*, 5.

quoted various people about Butler, appearing to accept all testimony, even when contradictory. Butler appears as a staunch defender of the faith of his devout Baptist mother, a shrewd antagonist to Confederate resistance, and the probable blackmailer of General Grant. Butler may have indeed been this complex a character, but Macartney does not reconcile these elements into a comprehensible portrait.

Macartney showed many positive qualities in his works. They were certainly not hagiography, covering the shortcomings of his subjects. Even those Macartney deeply admired, such as Lincoln, were revealed to have human foibles—although with Lincoln failures seem to be more often mistakes in judgment than flaws in character. Macartney was not naïve. He tried to quote fairly the individuals concerned, to allow them to present their own views. But he was also willing to critique—or at least express suspicion of—the comments that he quoted, such as discounting Seward's praise of Lincoln after the Chicago nominating convention, when his kind words were almost certainly not what Seward really thought.[83]

Finally, to return to the central question: how does a Fundamentalist write history? Macartney showed clear evidence of being a "Christian historian." His interest in Christianity affected his selection of material (e.g., constantly pointing out notes of piety), and he unashamedly cited providence in his larger evaluations. In a more subtle point, he insisted on Christianity as a force in history, shaping persons and events even if providence was not always acknowledged by the historical figures actually in the midst of events. He displayed character qualities in his writing that one would expect of someone professing the Christian faith: honesty, fairness, balance, and diligence—although these are, of course, qualities of any good historian. He added to character a pursuit of original sources, quoted and represented accurately. In this quality Macartney reflected a Christian heritage going back as far as Eusebius.[84] Macartney does not stand out in the field of Civil War history, but as the comments on his study of "Baldy" Smith demonstrate, he did at least make some original contribution. Havlik calls Macartney "one of the last non-professional historians to wade through and sort out the older available Civil War literature and data,

83. *Lincoln and His Cabinet*, 110–11.
84. The point here is that in earlier Greek historiography, literary license was generally acceptable. Few believe that the speeches in Thucydides, for example, are anything close to a transcription. Eusebius, in a Christian pursuit of truth, was a pioneer in digging out sources and quoting them fully and accurately—which is not to say that his sources were always accurate.

during a period when much of it consisted of biased autobiographies and reminiscences of aging survivors" and also "was one of the last authors to personally tramp through the old battlefields and historical sites while still untouched by commercialism and conservationists."[85] In short, Clarence Macartney offered a creditable body of popular work based on careful research and shaped by his definite Christian viewpoint. He showed that a "Fundamentalist" could be a historian—and could be a good one.

---

85. Havlik, "The Lincoln Civil War Books by Clarence Edward Macartney," 17.

www.ingramcontent.com/pod-product-compliance
Lightning Source LLC
Chambersburg PA
CBHW071510150426
43191CB00009B/1475